How to Own and Operate a Successful Small Business

What I Learned From 35 Years in Small Business

By

David Glick

Copyright 2018

G6 Publishing Co.

For my dad – without his devotion and help I would not be where I am today.
I am eternally thankful.

Contents

Preface 6

Introduction 8

Is This the Right Thing for You to Do? 15

Deciding What to Sell 20

Making the Transition from Job to Business 32

Time Management 37

Sole Proprietorship, Partnership, LLC, or Corporation? 42

Starting Your Business 47

The Real Secrets to a Successful Start 60

Buying Someone Else's Business 63

Branding and Marketing Your Business 68

    Part 1: Branding, Marketing, and Advertising 68

    Part 2: You have customers/patients/clients! Now what? 85

    Part 3: Reputation Management 89

    Part 4: Marketing Summary 97

Wearing Your 'Hats' 100

Employees - You Need Them to Make the Big Bucks 105

Restaurants: Risks and Rewards 128

Opening a Home-Based Business 140

Buying into a Franchise 144

Buying Into an MLM 149

What Do Your Customers See? 153

Brick and Mortar: Finding the Space 159

You Opened Your Business!! Now What? 170

The Most Important Piece of Customer Service 172

Owner Burnout 175

Billing and Getting Paid 179

Accounting for Your Business 182
Selling Your Business 186
Final Words - The Best Advice You May Ever Get 191
Great Resources 201

Preface

It took me well over 2 years to write this. I decided to write it in December 2015. Shortly after, my dad got very sick. He passed away in March 2016. It took me a long time to come to grips with his passing and get back to writing again. I am pleased to present to you my completed effort.

Why did I write this, yet another book on small business? Although there are tons of resources out there for small business and lots of people have written books on the topic, I felt that a book providing my detailed insight along with great information and personal experiences in one place would be very helpful, especially to the newer or budding small businessperson.

When I first got started in my pizza business, I needed answers, and I needed them fast. I ended up searching for years for a book like this one. There was none. I spent a ton of money on a very thick book about entrepreneurship and I thought that was my answer. It wasn't. Sure, it had some helpful info in it, but it was very boring reading and it did not hold the information that I was specifically looking for. What I was looking for IS in **this book** and that's exactly why I wrote it. I hope that you find it helps you as much as it could have helped me all those years ago.

Who this book is written for: If you are looking into starting your own business for the first time or even the 5th time and need focus and direction, this book is for you. Or, if you are already in business and looking for additional information and enlightenment on how to be more successful in your small business, this is DEFINITELY the book for you.

Introduction

NO ONE GOES INTO BUSINESS TO FAIL. To what degree do you agree with that statement?

Yet, the small business failure rate is astounding. Restaurants of course have the highest failure rate. Some estimates state that up to 80 percent of ALL small businesses fail in the first 5 years. Are you going into business to fail? To lose all that money you or someone else invested? To work all that time and put all that energy, blood, sweat, and tears into your baby just to **lose it**? Of course not! At least I hope not anyway!

You think it can't happen to you? I got news for you – the statistics don't lie. UP TO EIGHTY PERCENT OF SMALL BUSINESSES <u>FAIL IN THE FIRST FIVE YEARS</u>. Read that again... Do you get it? Whatever you do, do NOT think you are immune to failure! That will almost all but guarantee failure because you will probably NOT take the necessary steps to help prevent that failure.

But YOU can do something about it to improve your chances for success! **Read this book.** Understand it. Be coachable. Do what it recommends. I promise, better yet, I **guarantee** that it will improve your chances of success by more than you could **ever** know.

About me: I was born in 1960. This was just before color television came out (all television shows were in black and white!), well before personal computers were widely available, and nearly four decades before the Internet became a primary source of information and entertainment. I grew up in a suburb in northern New Jersey about 60 miles from New York City. Dad was a CPA (became fully self-employed when I was 11) and mom was a stay-at-home mom. Both of my grandfathers and some of my greats owned businesses, so you might say small business was in my blood.

My very first business was a lemonade stand. When I was about 8 years old I noticed that some kids would sell lemonade to thirsty people on hot summer days. I thought it would be fun. Maybe I could even make some money, as long as mom or dad sprung for the lemonade and cups. My mother made the lemonade and I stood outside for about 3 hours with the lemonade and cups on a TV tray. I sold one cup of lemonade. That was to my mother because she felt sorry for me. It was challenging waiting outside in the sun waiting for someone, anyone, to come along and buy. My mother was not in business at the time. She had no idea about marketing and advertising. So, she could not help me figure out how to get more business! At that point, I decided the lemonade business was not for me.

My second business was a lawn mower repair shop. I ran it out of my garage when I was about 15. Even as a young boy I wanted to know how things worked so I took things apart and (sometimes) was able to put them back together again. As a teen, I loved working on small engines and learned a lot about them by taking them apart and putting them back together. I fixed several of them on my own, so I decided to try fixing them for others. I went into partners with a friend because it sounded like fun. We made up some flyers and distributed them in the neighborhood. We got one customer – a neighbor across the street. He had an unusual type of lawn mower compared to what I had worked on. Although we fixed it, we spent way more time on it than we got paid for. We impatiently decided that the lawn mower repair business was not for us. I went on being a teenager.

More years passed. I went to work for my third Burger King when I was 19 and helped open a brand-new store with the owner and other employees. After some management attrition, I eventually moved into an assistant manager position. After a year and a half there I decided that I wanted my own restaurant. Although I was only 20 years old, I knew that I wanted to work for myself and not someone else.

I took some courses at the local community college which I aced and joined a college fraternity that is for budding entrepreneurs. Phi Beta Lambda is still in existence today and I do recommend it for any college student that wishes to learn more about the business of business. High school students can join Future Business Leaders of America and learn a ton about the business world! I went with the fraternity brothers to Portland, Oregon for an awesome business leadership conference. I learned a lot about business there, but it wasn't quite enough as I would find out soon enough.

I had talked to my dad about owning a business during that time. Knowing where my heart was, he helped me buy a pizza business from one of his clients. Dad lent me the money by taking out a second loan on his house. Yes, he had confidence in me. Maybe that was a bit misplaced in me for being only 20 years old, but I really wanted it. What did I know about pizza? Not much! I did have a little experience managing a convenience store. I also learned a lot about management, inventory, customer service, and other important business aspects at Burger King. Regardless of the little bit of practical experience I had, I wanted to do it anyway.

The previous owner trained me for 2 weeks before the closing date. Then the closing date came. I still remember it like it was yesterday: January 4, 1982. I had just turned 21 six weeks earlier. I was in for the shock of my life. I knew it would be difficult. I was taking over a place that used artificial cheese in the pizza. This is just an example of the poor-quality food being served. The teenage managers turned the dining room into a gaming room with a pool table right in the middle of the dining area. This tactic invited the high school kids with no money and scared away the adults that had any money at all. On top of that, this was during the tail end of the recession of 1980-1982. The small town in Arizona I lived in got hit hard, and no one had money to spend. It was miserable.

I cried a lot and bled a lot because I cut or burned myself more than once or twice. I even broke my hand once and my ankle another time. Yes, I was just in my early 20's! Somehow though, I was able to get past all the challenges and make it, especially thanks to my dad lending me more money when I really needed it. My ex-boss from Burger King came down the mountain one day and spent an afternoon with me. He offered me some great advice. I thank him for that because I really needed it at that time. I needed it more than anyone could ever know. Failure was not an option. My dad's house was on the line. My well-being was on the line too.

Finally, a very long 2.5 years later and after implementing many changes, I was able to say that my business was successful. I bought a new car after driving around in a horrid-mobile for 2 years. I took a vacation with my dad and step-mom and saw my grandma for the very last time. I also saw my future wife for the first time in 4 years (we dated in college). It was an awesome vacation and one that I will always treasure. Primarily because my then successful business was able to pay for it after all the stress, hard work and extreme worrying.

That pizza place was mine for 23 years. Some years I netted 6 figures. What I was able to do was amazing once I figured it out. It was extremely fortunate that I only had me to take care of in the early days. The barrel was scraped dry on many occasions; the bank account was in the red more than I would like to acknowledge. The postman even laughed at me once because he knew that I was getting all these NSF (Insufficient Funds) notices from the bank, and I sure did have to eat a ton of pizza in those days. I had some good days, but they were few and far between. Mostly it was stress and sweat. However, I persevered and figured it out – thank goodness before it was too late.

Over the years I started more businesses. Finally, I sold the pizza business to a manager after exactly 23 years. I own businesses to this day. I still have the entrepreneurial spirit and probably always will. I wrote this book because I want to pass on my experiences to you. It is my wish that it saves you from many of the difficult consequences I experienced due to the many mistakes that were made. This book will give you resources and knowledge that should save you many multiple thousands of dollars, hopefully making this book one of the more valuable resources in your current arsenal. It will not prevent you from making all mistakes. I can guarantee that. But - you will learn from those for yourself! I never said it would be easy. But this book WILL help! Businesses are in business for two reasons (generally speaking) – 1) To provide one or more needed products and/or services to people and 2) to make money. **If you don't have something to sell that people will buy, your business will not succeed.** With that said, I hope you enjoy this book as much as I enjoyed writing it for you.

NOTE: There are many 1000's of different niche businesses out there. It is beyond the scope of this book to address how to help with every possible type of business. I am certain that you will find gold nuggets in this book no matter what your niche is. I hope that the information you gather from my book and put to use every single hour of every single day will help you build a fortune in your small business!

Is This the Right Thing for You to Do?

> IN ANY MOMENT OF DECISION
> THE BEST THING YOU CAN DO
> IS THE RIGHT THING...
> THE NEXT BEST THING
> IS THE WRONG THING...
> AND
> THE WORST THING YOU CAN DO
> *IS NOTHING*
>
> – Theodore Roosevelt

You might think I am joking in asking that question. Seriously though, it takes a special kind of person to own a business. Or, should I say, it REALLY takes a special mind-set to own a business. Many people that want to own a business are not in that mind-set. To discover for yourself if this is doable for you, here is a list of questions you need to honestly answer for yourself:

1. Are you prepared to work 60-80 hours a week in your business, for up to 5 years or more? That doesn't mean you have to do this EVERY week, but MOST every week you may need to.

2. Are you prepared to accept that your business could fail, or that it could succeed beyond your dreams? How about a combination of both? Plans need to be made to address both possibilities.
3. Do you have money put away that you could live on for 3-6 months? Or, can you work a job around the time you must put into your business while your business gets up and running? Can you get a loan that could provide that security if needed? Keep in mind you must include the new loan payment in your monthly outgoing bills.
4. Is your significant other prepared for you to work the hours that you need to? Will he or she support your initiative 100%? How about facing the possibility of taking a financial hit if needed to support the business? Or, do you not have a significant other to worry about?
5. Do you have kids that you need to support? How will you support them during the very rough beginning times that could occur and last a year or more? What about child-care? Some parents have their kids with them while they run their business. Is that fair to them or to you? Your children, if old enough, must also understand that you may not be around as much as you have been.
6. Do you feel comfortable talking to people you don't know? If you don't, now is the time to get comfortable because you MUST talk to people when you own almost any business. You have NO

choice. In 90 percent of businesses, you must learn how to sell yourself and be confident in doing so.

7. Are you a people person (goes along with number 6, sort of)? Do you make friends easily? Do you know a lot of people already? If yours will be a local business, this will be a huge asset to you.

8. Do you have a talent or knowledge in a particular subject in life that can fill a need AND will earn you a living? Would that need be product based or service based, or both? You need to know this. If you don't, you need to learn one or you will not be successful. You may have a passion but if it does not fill a need that has demand and that people will pay for, your passion will not make a good business.

9. Are you willing to put 100% effort into the venture no matter what, at all times, and do whatever it takes legally to make it work? If you are not, you lessen your chances of success.

10. Are you willing to learn new ways of doing things? Can you accept that you don't know everything? How about knowing that there will be a HUGE learning curve in learning how to operate a business? You must be teachable, willing to expand your knowledge, and try new things. If not, you will greatly lessen your chances of being successful.

11. Do you like technology? If you don't, now is the time to make it a friend. Technology doesn't have to be your best friend. But believe me if you don't even own a computer, tablet, or smartphone you must get one – now. Technology runs our world.

Businesses that do not use it look antiquated to their customers. They also tend to be much less successful than those that use technology to their advantage. They will also run much less efficiently. Look at websites as well. You are going to need one unless your business is an MLM or one that doesn't require any Internet contact at all. You can hire a web designer, but you need to understand what a website can and cannot do for you. You could also do a funnel website (more on that in the website chapter).

12. Do you have a support team? A support team includes an accountant, a lawyer, and a business adviser or coach. You may need an adviser or friend that is knowledgeable about what you want to sell. If you don't have a support team, you must begin looking for members. They need to be knowledgeable, timely, and trustworthy.

13. Are you a leader? "A leader is the one who knows the way, goes the way, and shows the way." by John C Maxwell. This quote is a great example of leadership. You should consider this if you need to hire employees. I talk about employees in another section of this book. For now, though, know that many businesses cannot make serious money without them. Also know that without employees, there is only one person to run the business. That person is you - in sickness and in health. No one is always healthy. I got pneumonia when I was 22. I went to work in my restaurant anyway (pneumonia isn't contagious). Three weeks of agony but I

couldn't afford employees, and I couldn't very well close the place. Getting sick in business is a very tough spot to be in.

That's a very honest list, right? Read it again if you need to... If you cannot answer yes to most all of these questions, you should consider working for someone else. Really. You do not want to throw a bunch of money away. Investing in something that you do not love or that you are not willing to put the time into becomes miserable. I have been there - believe me. I have split-time between businesses, especially during the critical start-up time-frame. Know that this is difficult to do at best. If you aren't there to run the business, all kinds of issues WILL come up. What kinds of issues? Everything from employee theft to a complete lack of caring for your customers. Very low productive times are also a potential consequence. That means you are paying people to do little of what they are supposed to be doing.

There is no 50-50 here! You must throw yourself completely and 100% into the decisions you make. You must be willing to take complete responsibility for your actions and decisions. There will be rewards. There will be negative consequences. **Learning from both will be the keys to your success.**

Deciding What to Sell

Now that you have decided you would like to own and operate your own business, let's figure out what you want to sell. Is this going to be a product-based business or a service-based business, or a combination of both? Businesses that provide services usually provide products as well.

Examples of niches that provide products along with services include plumbers and electricians. Computer repair/IT and air conditioning repair are also included in this category. The products they sell are usually ancillary to their services. They can make some money selling products related to their services. Product-based businesses usually do not provide services to their customers although they can. Also, if the product can be warrantied for a time, extended warranties can be sold. This provides additional income through the warranty service (unless the product is low quality, and you really don't want to go there, right?). So, what is a restaurant? Is it a product or a service? Well according to one of my previous mentors, restaurants sell an experience. In other words, both! Always remember that - you aren't really selling what you think you are selling - what is it that you are selling? A solution? An experience?

Choose 2 or 3 types of things that you might want to sell. Discover what kind of demand there is for each one and what kind of gross profit there is for each. Look at what is actually selling and not just what the asking price is. The gross profit is the cost you sell it for minus the cost you bought it for. Narrow down and then focus on the winner - the ONE thing in the beginning. The Internet is a great resource, but it is also easy to get sidetracked and then you end up wasting time instead of being efficient with it. Be careful and stay focused.

Spreading yourself across multiple channels or over-complicating your efforts is not the way. KISS – Keep It Simple… Over-complicating things will not give you best chances for success. When I did the pizza business I learned that I needed to focus on pizza in the beginning. You must get your core product/service RIGHT and the BEST it can be –

then you can move on. When I did computer repair, I focused on computer repair in the beginning. When I did the TV/VCR repair we focused just on that. You can branch out later, based on customer inquiries and other input. But this is definitely not wise in the beginning unless you have people that can put their focus into being really good at additional things.

Do not try to be everything to everyone. This will guarantee that you are nothing to anyone.

What is the one interest that you have that sparks your passion? What are you good at? Can you make money at it? Have you fixed things before such as your car? What about things in your house such as electronics or appliances? Service-based businesses are big money-makers if you are personable and very good at it, and most are not going away anytime soon. Have you made things for other people? This can include jewelry, crocheted items, and knitted or sewed items. Perhaps you can consider a drop-ship business… Drop shipping is where you re-sell products to end users. You buy the products from the manufacturer or the middle man and ship it to the end user. These are just suggestions. Be careful that you don't decide to get into a business where the market is oversaturated. This is where there's not enough buyers for the number of sellers in that specific demographic/geographic and niche.

Demographics are things about the person – how old they are, married or single, what they eat, their occupation, where they hang out, etc. Geographic data is where they live along with generalities about that area such as income level, house style, and other community info. Niche is the specific product or service you are selling and where you are selling it – local, regional (usually state or other type of region), national, or inter-national. Consider the niche to be the smallest piece of the pie you can think of. Take for example a chiropractor. Did you know that chiropractors can focus on different body parts, and with different treatment methods? Each body part they focus on AND the way they treat it is its own niche. Make sense?

Getting back to the discussion... What did you like to do as a kid? Could that be a starting point for considering what to sell? Did you go to college for something and could that be an idea for you? Take the knowledge you have and determine what problem you can solve that a lot of people have. What can you do different or better than others? What could your unique selling proposition be? That is the one biggest thing that you do better or different than anyone else and is considered the advantage of doing business only with you.

Another point that you will want to explore while deciding what to sell is to make sure what you want to do is legal. Seriously – some people do not do the research to verify that what they are selling is legal! A few years ago, I helped a business owner establish what he considered to be a gaming facility. He told me his business would be where people could come in and play video games. What he withheld from me was that he was actually going to start a gambling gaming facility. He did not bother to check with local authorities, either!

He assumed it would be okay to do this because people do gamble on the Internet. Here in Arizona, it is legal to gamble on Indian land. But this was not Indian land and he is not Indian. Apparently without much consideration for these things, he rented his space (with a 3-year lease!). He paid for the utility deposits and ordered the Internet service. He bought the computers and networking equipment (from me) and had them installed. Finally, he got the legal entity name registered with the state and was all ready to open shop. The town came in and shut him down before he even opened the doors! Needless to say, he lost a bundle of money, all because he did not do his due diligence.

Are you considering going into a business that is not a mainstream business? If so, please verify you are not violating any laws or infringing on anyone's rights. Please do not spend all your time and money investing on this type of business without doing so. A lawyer or government office will be happy to squash it like a bug if you are out of line. Therefore, consult with them first, before doing anything else.

As I stated in my introduction, **a business is all about providing**

one or more products or services to people that have a need AND are willing to pay enough for it to make a profit. You provide solutions to problems. That's it. People are hungry - they want to eat - they also want a fun experience. Eating and fun experiences go together. They worked all day long and want to relax. They have kids that need things. They need things. They need to keep their cold food cold. They need to cook their food. They need to be clean. They need things fixed that break. They must get to work. They want their plumbing and air conditioning/heating system to work. They need restful sleep. They need to wake up. If they have a business, they have different needs. They need product suppliers and technical support. They need branding, marketing, and advertising help. Where does your product or service fit in?

The more that people have the need, the greater number of possibilities will exist for the business. If there are too many businesses in a market for the current demand, a new business's chances of success are slim. I previously brought up oversaturation - that's what this is. Please only consider this route if you have lots of money to burn and lots of patience. An exception to that rule is if your business (greatly) improves on current solutions. Keep in mind though that there is a finite amount of business in a niche. Improved product or service will likely mean that another business will not survive. If demand is high and the supplier selection for the product or service is slim, the odds of success are higher and higher prices can be charged. What is a product or service worth? Whatever a purchaser is willing to pay for them. That's how free enterprise works.

For example, when more competitors opened their doors, my pizza business slowed down. This especially occurred if they were a chain operation. That's because people are initially drawn to a national chain. Chains usually have great marketing power and can command a greater attraction. But when those chain operations went out of business, we became much busier. When Peter Piper Pizza closed their doors after 6 years in business, we began having record weeks. This was after 16 years of being in the business! Here is why they went out: they had a 5200 square foot location that they had trouble paying rent. Even though they brought in many 1000's of dollars of business every week, their 'housing' cost buried them. When they closed shop, other pizza restaurants in town benefited. This was a real boon for my restaurant at the time!

Getting back to the topic... After you have chosen one or more products or services, determine whether a market exists. Remember to stick to the ONE thing! Here are some questions to ponder. Is this something you will sell locally, on the Internet, or another medium? Will it be an international business? If so there are other considerations that you need to look at such as shipping prices. Can you compete with other businesses selling the same products? What if your shipping costs might be higher? Questions like that, hard and fast questions, need answers. If you cannot justify the costs of selling the product, then you are not going to make money. The business will fail.

How can you tell if a market exists for your product or service? Let's talk about a local business. This is a product or service that you will sell in the same town or city you live in, or the same state. The first thing to do is to look and see if other businesses offer the same products or services. Look at their prices. Determine if you can sell the same items for less money and still make money. Consider this though: price is not a good long-term strategy. It could help you in the beginning, though. What other competitive advantages can you offer that people care about enough to make a difference in your business? This is your unique selling proposition (USP). What other advantages can you offer to your customers if you cannot sell at a lower price?

What about the service aspect? Do the other businesses provide great service or can you improve on that? When I had my pizza restaurant we were the first one in town to offer pizza delivery. It took time to catch on. In the beginning I had to invent ways to make it worthwhile for both the driver and the restaurant. Delivery caught on after a while, and we had way more business than the places that would not deliver. Pizza Hut finally started delivering as well because they didn't want to get left behind. This is an example of how you can improve your service over your competition.

Here is a second example from the pizza business. I computerized the operation in 1993 - WAY back when 😊. After the initial learning period, we were able to get off the phone with customers in 30 seconds or less, even with delivery orders. This was just the beginning of the computer age, so it amazed people we were able to do that so quickly. We asked for their phone number, and up popped their name (so we could call them by name), address, last orders, etc. It literally would only take us a few seconds to put their order in, confirm their address, and tell them when we would be there, versus the 1-2 minutes it had previously taken to hand-write all the orders. We were WAY ahead of ALL our competition in terms of service! The other benefits of course were that orders were more accurate, and our productivity went way up because one person could handle more phone orders in less time.

A huge advantage us little guys have over the big guys is that we can change our business model on a dime. We want to start pizza delivery within 5 days? No problem! We get whatever equipment we need for the service. We figure out transportation, insurance, etc. Then we determine the process, hire a driver or two, and start delivering! Say we hire a guy that shows us how to make this cool dish and we want to add it to the menu? No problem! We begin serving it as a special and have new menus printed up, ready in a week or less, and voila - new dish is on the menu. Those things really happened, by the way!

The big guys cannot even begin to match the little guy's swiftness to market. The small business has huge advantages in bringing products and services to market. Always remember that. Determine the need. Make the plan. If you know in your heart it will work, follow it through. Make the change! You can always go back if you need to. One caveat: if it requires a large investment... Test the idea with a small but very representative audience first before making the leap. Oh, and by the way, following the competition is not necessarily a smart way to compete. You want to be the market LEADER, not the FOLLOWER. If you know what you do better, then exploit it!

I digressed just a bit – back to the topic at hand. What we want to sell needs a market! We cannot sell what we consider to be a perfectly good product or service to no one. One way to figure this out in a local market is to perform a survey. Talk to your friends and relatives – do they see a need for it? Would they buy it? Okay seriously though. Don't rely only on your friends or relatives because unless they have a mean streak. they may support anything you do! Talk to LOTS of other people. Talk to the cashier at the convenience store you go to, the gas station, and your hairdresser or barber. You don't need to give all the secrets – just a general idea of what it is that you wish to sell.

You get the picture! Find out everything you can. Ask whether they would buy it or use it, how much they would pay for it, and if they would refer their friends. Sometimes you can even stand outside a store and ask people for their opinions. Ask the store's permission first! Let them know what you are doing and how long you will do it for. You can also make a survey on the Internet. Surveymonkey.com as of this writing provides free survey capabilities. Email it to people you know that are in your target market and look at the results. Make sure they are in your target market! Attempting to sell senior citizens a bicycle might not generate much interest.

Now that you have considered what to sell and determined there is a market for it, you need to figure out the costs. How much will it cost you to buy, to make, and to package, and how much can you sell it for. Do not leave anything out! When I first got into the pizza business, I decided that the pizza boxes were so cheap I didn't factor them into my costs. That applied to a few other things, too! Big mistake – my costs ended up being so high because those things added up (and quickly at that!). I had to re-factor everything I was selling and change my prices. I had to do that to cover my costs!

If you are not selling your products for enough money, you will not be able to pay your costs and you will not make a profit. So again, factor EVERYTHING into your base costs.

If you are selling a service, you cannot sell yourself short. Undercutting your competitors sounds like a great idea at first. But, the

ONLY reason to do so is if you are very new to the industry. You will still face a huge learning curve. I did that in the beginning with my computer repair business. Not knowing as much as my competitors, I took longer for repairs. So, I charged less per hour. I still guaranteed the repair. If I couldn't fix it, I didn't charge. Although my hourly income suffered compared to competitors, I learned a lot. My knowledge eventually became far superior to most of my competitors. As I learned increasingly more about my craft, my services became more expensive. My quality of service more than justified the price increases. I knew more than my competitors and got the job done faster!

Now - do you know what you want to sell? Did you verify there is a market for it and that you can cover your costs (in a perfect world)? Let's move on……

Making the Transition from Job to Business

Do you currently have a full-time job that pays the bills? Are you are looking at moving into your own business? Then you have some considerations to think about. Your first thought should be: when should you make the transition from job to business? Let me tell you... It is going to be difficult to work a full-time job and start a business. You will work many hours. That could be very frustrating for you. You will not have the time to spend on your project that you want to. You may also be daydreaming of your new business while working your old one. Because of these things, you will want to make the transition as soon as you can. But, do not do this until you are quite certain that the business is and will remain profitable. Leaving the financial security of your full-time job too soon could be problematic.

Your hours could double or even triple. you may feel exhausted at times and you may want to give up. Therefore, proper planning is going to be a very important aspect of moving into your new business. If the business is home-based, then you can certainly work it in your spare time. But you cannot be in two places at once, such as if you are opening a brick and mortar. In that case, you have two choices: 1) Quit or cut down on your job, or 2) Hire employees. Neither one of those will work if you need the income from your job while your business is ramping up. That is a bad thing! An employee may cost you more than what you take in from your business, for example.

There came a time when I had the pizza business that I told my wife I wanted to sell it – I was sick of it and wanted out – BADLY. She told me there was only one way that was going to happen. *That was to figure out another source of income.* I pondered that for quite a while. Finally, some events occurred in my life that allowed me to move into my other business. That business took over my income needs, finally. It **only** took 7 very long years.

Yes, it was a long time and I am sure it could have happened in less time. But as you may discover for yourself, it is very challenging to run one business while ramping up another. Plus, I had to find a way to move the restaurant in the middle of all that! My proprietor sold the building to the guy that owned the carpet place in my complex. The new owner then wanted to use my space for his business. That didn't exactly help speed my plans of exiting the pizza business.

Needless to say, it was a rough 7 years. By the time I was able to finally sell the restaurant I didn't want to spend another minute in it. I was burnt out (discussed in another chapter) and I had no interest in the pizza business any longer. Remember that the restaurant business is one of the most difficult businesses to own. This is due to many reasons. These include the hours you must put into it, plus the quality of employees that you will find to hire. Not to mention the little nuances in knowledge and care that you need to make it and keep it successful. After getting the computer business running at decent clip, I sold the pizza business – this was 2005. Then the recession of 2007 hit. Another recession, another story....

Some events in my life told me the recession was coming. I could feel it in my bones (you really need to be in-tune with this stuff when you own a business and consider how it might affect you). Then the computer business began showing signs of the slow-down. This would soon prove to be one that our generation had not ever experienced.

I was not about to take any chances of a failure. Therefore, in 2007 I decided to work for another company - for the first time in a quarter-century. I applied for and was offered a job at the then number 3 cable company in the USA. It had great benefits but because I was an entry level worker my pay was quite low. The good thing was they offered overtime. I was no stranger to that, being in my own businesses for such a long time! I also made a lot of friends there and it was cool to be able to relate to people without being their boss.

After almost 3 years though, Corporate America disgusted me. I will admit that it was my attitude more than anything. I can lead or follow, but the leadership must be spot on, which due to certain inside politics it wasn't. Pretty typical for big companies. **SIDE NOTE:** Do your best to eliminate drama and politics at your small business. Always remember you have one priority – the success of your business. Drama and politics will usually derail those efforts.

Regardless of what was going on, it was time for me to take my leave. So here I was with a full-time job and wanted to start my business - again! I started my business before I quit the cable company - I knew I would get into it again; it was a matter of when. I accelerated the process after I determined that the time had come. I also had a new weapon to use in marketing - Search Engine Optimization and the Internet.

I saved up enough cash to live on for a couple of months. In retrospect, I really should have saved more. I went full time into the computer repair business again. Of course this was not my first rodeo. I knew what to do and how to execute so it was not as challenging as when my first business was growing. Not only that, but this was a home-based business so there was no rent and no employees to pay in the beginning.

My primary point here is this: **look at the big picture.** You need to have a Plan B ready to go at any time. I live to that mantra and believe that it is super important to do that. If you have never thought about a Plan B you really need to. It could help you out of a sticky situation one day. You don't have to write it down, but you should remember it. Plan B – make one today.

The process of moving from a job to a business or from one business to another is called side-hustle. See the resource guide at the back of this book for a great article on Side Hustle.

Time Management

You may have heard this term in the past, and you may have wondered what it meant or how to apply it. Or, it didn't mean anything at all to you. Either way, time management is one of the most important concepts as a business owner that you will need to know. Get to understand it and master it. If you do not do this, you will be wasting time on tasks that will not be productive. Tasks that ARE productive to your business either will not get completed or delayed. This will not be helpful to you, possibly until it is too late. Time management will help you hit your target and achieve your goals in a timely manner (pardon the pun!).

As you may have gathered from the previous paragraph, you must manage your time in relation to tasks. You need to work tasks every day. Setting goals and achieving those goals requires that you complete certain tasks. Each task that you complete should result in a movement toward your goal. Complete your tasks. Take incremental steps every hour of every day until you achieve each goal. Then begin the process all over again for a new set of goals.

What is the best way to achieve goals? First, determine what those goals are. Write them down and look at them every day. Write a list of activities every day that will help you work toward your goals. Know this - you will not be perfect at this, especially in the beginning. You may underestimate your available time. You may get everything done quicker than you expected. You may have less time than you expected and some of your tasks will not get completed as expected.

That's okay. Time management experts say that if you have more time, take the rest of the day off. Then get back to it the next day. If you didn't complete your tasks, be sure to complete the MOST important ones first. When you make your list, put the most important tasks first and complete them first. Then work on the less important tasks. Add any incomplete tasks to the following day's list.

When I was in the pizza business, one of my goals early on was to average $500 a day in sales. That may seem like a small goal for a restaurant. But when the business hadn't even achieved that goal in any one day of sales, that does become a rather lofty goal! But, I did set that goal for myself, and I wanted to make it happen. I did that. It took well over a year, but it did happen. After I achieved that goal, my next goal was $1000 a day average.

All goals need a proper plan. Work on executing that plan every day. I made my original goal happen by figuring out what I needed to do. First, I had to be sure I had the capacity. Based on the then current sales, I figured out approximately how much more of everything I needed to sell. Then, according to how the business came in, I had to make sure I ordered the proper amount of inventory. Then I had to verify that we could make enough food at a time to keep the customers happy. I also figured out how many employees I would need to keep up with the demand at that sales level.

TIP... When running a special in a product business, verify that you have the capacity and inventory to fill all customer orders quickly. There is almost nothing worse than running a great special and then running out of product too fast. An even worse problem would be giving very slow service! You will lose money. Customers can and WILL walk out. You will upset your (new) customers. They may never come back.

The first impression is the most important impression. Not making a good impression will cause you grief. That is the exact OPPOSITE of what you were trying to do. Plan - plan and plan some more. After all that planning, have a smart plan B.

Next, I had to make the plan (remember the last sentence?) - how would I increase my clientele by the amount needed to reach that $500 a day average? There are several ways to increase sales in a business - they include:

* Increase the number of people purchasing from you

* Increase the average order (in the restaurant business this is known as ticket average)

* Increase the number of times the average customer orders from you.

Your best chance of increasing sales is not to use one of these techniques, but all of them! That is what we did. We employed a combination of techniques that increased the number of people purchasing from us. We used several mass-media and guerrilla marketing techniques for this. We increased the average ticket order by raising prices somewhat. This worked well because we were way underpriced in our market anyway. Plus, we added more menu items that enticed our customers to buy more food. Because we added more menu items, people came more often to buy from us. Then we instituted a customer appreciation program. The more that customers purchased from us, the faster they would earn an award.

As you can see, the 3-pronged approach to increasing sales works well, but it takes focus and discipline to use it. All employees must be on board for this but may not because you are increasing their workload too. Convincing them this is the best thing for the business should not be too difficult. Restaurants are stressful to work in. Making sure your staff is adequate at all times helps to keep stress levels as minimal as possible. Remember to account for no-shows and other attendance issues. Those can be quite a challenge but are very important.

Here is the news. If you have good time management skills, then you may achieve your goals in a shorter time-frame. However, not having those time management skills and will extend the time required to achieving goal. As I write this book I find that my time management skills still need sharpening occasionally. It is not something that you learn and then forget about. You must keep after it and refresh those skills sometimes. Your business depends on it. And yes, we also achieved the $1000 a day goal :)

Sole Proprietorship, Partnership, LLC, or Corporation?

First, a disclaimer – I do not intend to provide legal or accounting advice here. Please seek the advice of your tax and legal professional for any of these matters!

Here are the primary types of business ownership in the United States:

The Sole Proprietorship is your business. Only one person owns it and only one person is legally responsible for it. Advantages include the fact that there is only one person. You are the only boss. It is easy to make changes to the both the business itself and the structure of the business. Legal filings are generally simple. Currently in the USA, you'll file a Schedule C with your tax return to show the profit or loss of the business for the tax year. Disadvantages of the sole proprietorship include full liability for all legal issues. Such issues include any that may arise out of doing business. This includes the legal system having full access to the owner's finances should someone decide to sue you. **TIP: Look into an Umbrella Insurance Policy.** Also, you could end up paying more in taxes than with a LLC or corporation when your business makes you a living.

The Partnership (general, limited, or limited liability) requires at least 2 people. Partnerships have many advantages. They are easy to form and rather easy to manage compared to other company types. You can make changes to the business without having to go through formal proceedings. much like the sole proprietorship. One primary problem with partnerships are that they can be difficult to dissolve. The more partners there are, the more complicated things get. Usually each partner has a share of the profits. Things can get rather sticky if things go sour between some or all partners. Liability can also be an issue. Limited liability partnerships can limit the legal liability of the partners. You may also pay more in taxes with a partnership than with a LLC or corporation. You will need to file a Partnership Agreement with your local government agency. This describes who you are, what you will do, and how things will run. Get a lawyer to help you with the agreement. When things are good, they are good but when things are bad, they can be REALLY bad. **TIP: I do NOT recommend going into business with a partner, ANY partner, unless you have a VERY compelling reason to do so. Friends ESPECIALLY should not go into business together. It may not seem bad now, but many previously good friendships have been erased due to business matters.**

A LLC (Limited Liability Company) has a lot of advantages for small businesses. They receive the tax and liability advantages of a corporation. You must file as a Sub-chapter S to gain some of the tax advantages. Seek out your tax professional for advice on this BEFORE establishing the LLC! LLC's have great advantages; they can be small and easy to manage. As of this writing they also do not have the filing and meeting requirements of corporations. Many small business owners opt for the LLC designation for several reasons. These include the relative simplicity, low startup costs, and ease of doing business. Again, seek out the advice of your trusted legal counsel and accountant regarding the liability and tax aspects of the LLC.

The Corporation has at least one owner, depending on the state - so please check yours. But, you can incorporate in a different state than you live in. There are also different types of corporations. Advantages of the corporation include limited liability for the owners in most cases. But, there are exceptions to this so check with your lawyer. Another advantage is that owners can change easily. The corporation has a board of directors. Shareholders vote in the directors. The Articles of

Incorporation determine how often board meetings take place. Meetings generally must take place at least yearly. They may be held more often to elect the board and take care of other business issues. Corporations can be challenging to run. Corporate profits are usually double-taxed unless it is a Subchapter-S . Taxation occurs once to the corporation, and once to the individual shareholders.

There is one more type of business – the non-profit. The non-profit's purpose is not to make money unlike the other business types. It's purpose, for example, may be helping people. Other purposes include helping animals or the environment, as primary examples. This could be for health care, senior care, care for the poor, or help or care for those unable to care for themselves. Other instances include educating people, providing recreational activities, or churches and synagogues. The business's aim is not to make a profit but to exist for its purpose(s). Also, as a rule anyone involved in the business are volunteers. The only exception to that rule is for those administering it. Non-profits still must raise money somehow to pay expenses.

They must rent a building, pay utilities, and pay other business costs. They also need to pay administrative salaries. As far as I know there is no salary limit for the administration, but they do need to be set every year. Non-profits do not get taxed because there is no profit. But, salaried administrative employees will pay taxes as ordinary income. If the business does make a 'profit,' the money generally must be designated for a specific purpose. Purposes can include purchasing a building or donating to a charity. Other purposes include helping with the organization or performing a social function. Other advantages to non-profits include reduced rates for costs associated with doing business. This includes procuring computers and software from larger companies. You can search to discover which companies provide discounted rates for non-profits. Large companies may also donate products and services to the non-profit.

How do you decide which form of organization is right for you? Unless you have a compelling reason to use another form, you should start out as a sole proprietor. I say this from my personal experience. I learned a lot from starting businesses on a shoestring. For example, if you have a partner you will want to explore another form of organization such as an LLC. That does not mean you cannot change later. If you find that your business is successful, you may opt for a different form of organization. Tax advantages, as I mentioned earlier, are a very good reason to change. It is always a good idea to transition into a LLC or a S-Corp because of the liability advantages. LLC's can file with S-Corp status - talk to your accountant. But in the beginning – the sole proprietorship will usually work best.

Starting Your Business

Before we go further, let's go over a short checklist. Did you:

1. Decide what you are going to sell?

2. Do the research to help make sure all the hard work you are about to put into your new business will not go down the tubes? You do not want to lose everything you currently own! This can

happen because you are selling something that not enough people want or is illegal.

3. Decide how you want to organize your business?

Yes? Great!! Now we can move on to the meat of what you have proposed. This is going to be another checklist of tasks that you should go through, in the order that you need to perform them. You will not be able to move on to the next item for some of them until you complete the previous task. IMPORTANT - READ THIS ENTIRE SECTION AND UNDERSTAND IT BEST YOU CAN BEFORE YOU START. There is a ton of important information here and there isn't a specific order to the whole thing. With that said, here we go – feel free to cross them off as you complete them!

BRICK AND MORTAR BUSINESSES:
a. You first will need to find a place to rent. You need to decide how big of a place you want. This includes the layout of the space and where you will rent as well as whether you can afford it. The 3 most important aspects of a space to rent which will determine the success or demise of your business are LOCATION, LOCATION, and finally, LOCATION. The first time I read this in a marketing book I thought it was meant to be a joke. It is not. If your customers do not want to drive to your space, you will not have a business. There are other considerations for the location as well.

For example, will you own a restaurant that sells liquor or a bar? In many states you cannot be within a certain distance of a school or church. How is the parking and is there enough for what you want to do? Location may be great, but it won't be good if your customers cannot find a convenient place to park. They may be unable to patronize your business. Is it a difficult walk? Is there handicapped access? If not, you may be liable to put it in. **IMPORTANT TIP!! If you locate in a mall or shopping center, don't rely on foot traffic unless it is very heavy.** Each business will make or break itself. In the space itself, what do the floors and walls look like? Is everything up to code? Is heating/cooling available if needed? Do the water heater and other appliances work? Are the restrooms handicapped accessible? Again, if not, you could be liable to make them that way. What kind of utilities service the building and are you happy with that? Do yourself a FAVOR and verify the address with the utility companies so there are NO surprises! If you want to start a restaurant, see the chapter under restaurants. There is so much more to consider that it requires a treatment of its own!

b. Once you find a space and are positive it is the best one for you, discuss the lease with the landlord. I strongly recommend you hire a lawyer to go over the lease and make changes in your favor. There is only one entity the original lease will favor. It will not be you. Everything is up for negotiation, even the price. Be tough but know when to back off and when they are bluffing. You have the upper hand except in high-demand areas. So, let them know they are not the only game in town, even if you aren't yet considering anywhere else. While you are in lease negotiations, you can move to the next steps. Consider when you are going to open the business too. Once that rent bill starts coming in you will be counting the days until you open! Make your lease start date work for you regarding your opening day. Give yourself enough time to remodel and spruce the place up. Look at replacing flooring or whatever else you need to get done.

ALL BUSINESSES:

1. Decide on a name for the business. **TIP: Learn BRANDING** (go to https://www.g6digitalmarketing.com/my-account/members-area/1239/my-membership-content/ - this is one of my websites - sign up for and take the branding course)! You will give yourself a competitive edge if you do - guaranteed. You will need a name for your entity if you will be organizing as anything but a sole proprietorship. The business name is also known as the dba (doing business as). For example, if you were Joe Block Sole Proprietor and your business name was Joe's Plumbing, you would be Joe Block dba Joe's Plumbing. If you were Joe Block LLC doing business as Joe's Plumbing, you would be Joe Block LLC dba Joe's Plumbing. You will not usually put both names like that on

any application or form. Most applications have the entity name and business name on separate lines. I wanted you to understand how to read it and understand it. Please refer to the asterisk in Step 4 for further information in the naming process. Understand that other businesses may already use the name you want. You have to know whether this is the case, so you will need to research that name! **TIP: Put your business niche IN YOUR NAME. How else will people know what you do?**

2. You will need to register your business with the federal authorities. You will need a Federal Tax ID Number if you are anything but a sole proprietorship. In this case your SSN will be your Tax ID. You can apply for this online – search "Apply for federal tax ID" and make sure you go to the real IRS site. Do not go to some bogus place wanting to charge you. The application is free from the IRS in the United States. Other countries will have different procedures so please consult with your trusted tax adviser or accountant. Next, if you will have employees at any time in the near future you will also need to register as an employer. **Do yourself a favor and let a reputable accountant do all tax registrations for you. It will get done right the first time. You will not have to worry about it!

3. You can open your business checking account after you get the Federal Tax ID and register with the state. Research this because

some banks will cost you less than others. Bank charges can add up. Find out how much it costs for the account maintenance fee every month. Look at how much they charge for deposits and if you can avoid those charges. Sometimes depositing through an ATM costs nothing for example. Ask how much the bank charges for NSF fees and how much they charge when a customer bounces a check. Are you considering accepting credit cards for payment? Ask the bank if they provide credit card processing and what it will cost. I learned a good lesson the first time I took credit cards in my business in 1991. I went with some salesman that came to my restaurant. He was advertising a low fee and a great processing machine. I was happy to start processing credit cards! The downside was the expense. I got locked into a 3-year contract which ended up costing me over two thousand dollars for the $500 machine. Do yourself a favor. Don't sign a long-term (3 year for example) contract for merchant services. Find another processor if they make you sign a contract longer than a year. There are tons of credit card processing providers out there that do not have contracts such as Stripe, PayPal, and Square. Square for example has entire POS systems dedicated to small business. They are not cheap, but their stuff works, and they use very good equipment. Speaking of equipment, many times you can find it on eBay or Amazon for a great price. Make sure the machine you buy is up-to-date on all compliance. Also verify compatibility with your processor.

4. Next, you will need to register with the state authorities. Sole proprietors usually don't need to register the name with the corporation commission. Again, please consult your legal and tax advisers on this info. I am not responsible for giving incorrect information for your state or country. **Yet you will still want to register your fictitious name with your state government in the US. Other countries may have a different process. This does two things – it verifies that you are the only one doing business as that name in your state. Also, it protects you from someone else taking that name. If they do, you will have a legal foot to stand on. Will you be doing business country-wide or you are competing against national chains? You may want to consider getting a federal copyright for your name. Again, if in another country, get the equivalent of that in your country. Are you organized as a LLC or corporation? Then register with your state's corporation commission. The commission authority in your state may have a different name. Will you be selling a product? You will need to get a sales tax license (also known as TPT - Transaction Privilege Tax). Verify with your state that there is no sales tax on services. If there is, then you will still need the TPT. If you have employees, you will need to register with the state as an employer. Also, check to verify your business name is NOT already registered in your country!

5. You will need to register with your local authorities. If you are doing a brick and mortar business in an incorporated area you will probably need a business license, for example. You may not if you are working out of your home, unless you are selling to local people. In that case, you might. Always check with your local authorities to make sure. You do not want to get yourself in trouble! Brick and mortar businesses may want to contact your local police department. This way they know who the owners are and give them your best reachable phone number in case of a break in. Those late-night calls are never fun. But, it's better to get the call than to discover the break in the next morning. Trust me.

   Are we having fun yet? Making good progress? Great!! Let's keep going!

6. BRICK AND MORTAR BUSINESSES: After your lease has been signed, you will pay the first month's rent and/or security deposit. You may have other payments due for your space so pay them as well. Then get the power, gas, water, septic, and telephone turned on as needed. Also, order things like Internet and Cable TV service as it suits your business. If you do not have commercial credit with the utility, you may need a deposit. Those deposits can add up to a lot of money. They are much higher in extremely hot or cold geographic areas or for a restaurant. It is also time finalize

the opening date! Be reasonable. I know that once that rent bill starts, you will be pushing to get the place opened up. Have a plan B that you can easily execute if Plan A doesn't go as planned :)

7. If your business is product based or you sell any products, you will need suppliers of either the finished products or raw materials. You will also need to establish protocols and procedures for your business. If you will have a lot of computer-based data, for example, then you will need a backup and disaster recovery plan. You will need to determine open and closed hours. Determine the days you will close. Establish a cleaning schedule and a stocking schedule, etc. TIP: Get a Gmail address if you don't have one. Then register your business on Google Maps (aka Google Business). Add your hours and your business description. Put in your niches and pictures of yourself, your store inside and out, and your goods if you have them. Do this about a month before you open. Google requires sending a postcard to the service address to verify the business. Then your business will have taken a huge step toward its important online presence. Home based service businesses should also register with Google as stated above.

8. Make sure that you know and understand every aspect of your business. Even if you will have employees, you are still the leader and you will need to do the training. An exception is if you hire a

very expensive manager to do that for you. That manager needs to have the knowledge of your business niche. But, if you lose that manager, what will you do if you do not have the knowledge to run the business? Ultimately the fate of your business rests with you! You will want to learn as much as you can about the business so your chances of being successful are as high as they can be! It will make the most sense for you and give you the best chances of survival.

9. You will need to establish prices for everything your business sells. Regardless of whether it is a product or a service, WRITE THEM DOWN. You cannot change your prices as your mood strikes. A big part of being in business is establishing a positive rapport with your customers. You want them to buy from you on a regular basis and you want them to spread the word about your business. But they will not like it if you change your prices every day. You must be a TRUSTED provider. As a rule, products sell for between 2 and 4 times what you pay for them wholesale, depending on the product. It depends on what you sell. Free market products and services sell for whatever the market will bear. High-end or high-ticket products may have to sell for less than 2 times wholesale value. Computer and electronics equipment? Forget about it! You will be lucky to increase your wholesale cost by 50% on most items, even less on many. If you can find a product to sell that is in high demand but has low competition you can make lots of

money. Popular products in highly competitive markets will usually not net you lots of money. What many businesses do is undercut everyone else in the beginning. This strategy gets people 'in the door' and begin establishing relationships. The business then increases prices later. What you do in your business is up to you. Always remember that if what you are doing is not working, you can always change. That's the beauty of being a small business!

10. Hire employees if you need them. There is a whole chapter on employees. You will discover tidbits on hiring, managing, and firing. Go look at it if you wish, then come back. Seriously :-)

11. Advertise your opening! If you are a brick and mortar business, you may not want to do this right away. You may opt for a 'soft opening'. This is where you open the doors and put an a-frame sign outside. Whoever shows up, shows up. This way you do not get bombarded with business that you cannot handle. On the other hand, you may be ready for a big turnout and you can handle it. In that case you will want to not only advertise the heck out of it but also put teasers out ahead of time. Also have your employees hand out flyers to everyone they know. They will do that. They may need a little carrot. Remind them that if the business is not successful they will not have a job.

12. BRICK AND MORTAR BUSINESSES: Verify you have done everything to be ready for your opening! You have your lights and other utilities on. The place is clean and looks and smells great (but not offensive). You have employees ready to go. They are knowledgeable about everything they need to know to do their job. They have practiced and are proficient. You have advertised your opening, so people will know about it. All the equipment is operating, including your technology! You have rehearsed the opening! Whoa - what??!! Yes! Rehearse the opening. You need to know where the kinks and service bottlenecks are as much as possible. Have some friends or relatives come and visit your store. Do this a day or two before you are set to open and have them 'buy' things from you. This is especially true for a restaurant. You could give an entire meal away to important business people in town. This is a great way to advertise your business and it will help ensure staff are ready to meet the demand. This will not guarantee it of course. It will help, however!

13. HOME BUSINESSES: Most of these same things apply. But, you are not going to get any foot traffic like you would in a storefront setting. You typically will only get business by advertising in a few ways. Word of mouth, flyers or brochures, radio, television, newspaper, magazine are some examples. You will also benefit from having your own website! Home based businesses are the least expensive to run because you are not paying rent. Utility

costs are shared in your home, but home businesses can also be costly to advertise. You don't get to use signs of any kind for your home unless it zoned for commercial. See the chapter on Marketing Your Business. It's super important!

The Real Secrets to a Successful Start

You may be wondering – what is the real secret to a successful start in business? You can do all the research. You can go through all the steps in the previous chapter. You can hire the best employees and have all your ducks in a row. Then 3 or 6 months later you find that you spent a whole lot of money. Yet, you are not paying the bills and you are sinking. It happens – trust me. You would not be the only one. The Small Business Association says that 20 percent of new businesses fail in the first year. More than fifty (50) percent fail in the first 5 years (some sources put this figure at up to 80 percent)! What could have happened? What went wrong and where?

Here are two separate yet very valid points to look at:

1. You may not have gone into a business that you have a passion for AND that can make enough money to be successful. If you do not have a passion for what you are doing, you are not going to be the best you can be at it. It is that simple. You must find a way to be passionate about what you are doing. You must be passionate about the subject matter itself AND what you need to do to run the business. Sure, you are not going to be passionate about every single aspect of the business. Many of us do not like having to write those checks to pay the bills every month. Many of us do not get or like marketing and have trouble figuring it out, as

examples. But you still must do those things to be successful – so find a way to discover a passion to do those things. When you signed up for this job you agreed to wear many hats – and that you must!

2. The second and even more valuable point is this – start SMALL!! You may have these feelings that you want to be big – real big. For example, having a 200+ seat steakhouse in the middle of a 10,000-population small town. But if the market doesn't support it, it will never succeed. Always start small, even if you are in the middle of a 2,000,000-population city. I repeat - no matter what you think – always start as small as you can.

If you need a $30,000 piece of equipment to start off with but are considering 2 pieces, wait. I promise! You will know if you need that second one soon enough. The machine company salesperson will always be happy to sell it to you. If you are a brick and mortar business, what kind of lease terms can you negotiate? Stay away from the 10-year lease until you know it will work. Go for a 2 or 3-year term lease that is renewable for a longer term if you can. Figure out how to keep your initial costs as low as you can, WITHOUT sacrificing anything. Product quality, service, and cleanliness are critical to your customer's satisfaction. 9 times out of 10 you can make the upgrades later. Start small, start inexpensive, and your chances of success will greatly improve.

Take it from someone that is an expert at starting businesses 'on a shoestring.'

I went into the television repair business with a really good friend in the late 1990's. This was while I had the pizza business. My friend loved the TV repair business as he had done it before, and I was very interested in it as well because I had a background in electronics. We started the business out of my garage until we had the income to pay rent and utilities on a place. We then shared a small 300 square foot space with a related electronics business. The TV repair business never lost money. That strategy worked great. We stayed in business until LCD and plasma televisions became popular a few years later. Do you see how the start small strategy in a business that you have a passion for can work best for you? What could have happened if we got into a commercial space with a rent fee of $500 a month or more? We wouldn't have had the time to build up the business. The business could have gone broke before it even had a chance for success.

Buying Someone Else's Business

A potential way to go into business for yourself is to buy someone else's existing business. This is a turn-key operation, known for that term because all you do is turn the key on the front door. Then turn on the lights, and BOOM! You are in business - if you remembered to put all the utilities in your business name :). Here are things to think about before making a final decision to buy the business. Most of these apply strictly to local brick and mortar businesses. But some are for all businesses, so read it through to discover what will apply to you:

1. Is this the exact business you want? Take a good hard look at the operation. Make sure that this is something that you can and want to do and that you have a passion for. Remember earlier I told you to know and understand all the operations of the business? And that you have a passion for it? It still holds true here!

2. Is it the right price? You will want to look at the books of the business. Some businesses, although illegal, have '2' sets of books. You will want to see both, and you will want proof that the income on the 'other' set of books is real. Hang out across the street for a few hours during their 'busy' time. Do this for a few days if you have the time. Count the customers going in and out of the door and see what they might walk out with. Restaurants

for example have something called an 'average ticket'. You can multiply the number of tables or takeout orders by the average ticket. Some businesses are seasonal so this may be more difficult to discover. Another litmus test is to look at the purchases the business has made for a product-based business. Their inventory and purchases made will help you discover what they actually sell. Some businessmen will even pay their suppliers in cash to hide the paper trail. So think about how this could affect the numbers. Service businesses may have a database on a computer with their customer's paid services. This is especially important for their warranty work, so look there.

3. Why is the owner selling? Ask him or her. He may say that he is ill or wanting to retire or wants to move or move on. Those are valid reasons. However, the real reason may be because he is going broke running the business. What are the current national and local economic conditions and is this a reason? Next, we will want to look at the business's reputation.

4. Ask people around the town about the business. Have they heard about it? Have they experienced it (was it good or bad)? If not, what is their feeling about the business? Have they heard good things or bad things about it? ALL BUSINESSES: Look online for reviews about the business. Type the name of the business in the

Google search engine, the name of the town or zip code, and the word "review." You should find everything you need to know.

5. If the business has a bad reputation, is it something that can be fixed in a short time? Is the business priced at the bottom because it has a bad rep? Local businesses that have a bad reputation can take up to two years or more to recover from that. It doesn't happen all at once, but to completely get over it the new owner should expect a recovery time that long. You will have to make the decision whether it is worth the risk to try and absolve a bad reputation.

6. Examine the lease. You must approve of all terms. The landlord also must approve you to take over the lease. If the existing business is currently month to month, you will want to negotiate a new lease. Month to month means that the landlord can ask you to leave at any time, with a 30-day notice. That is far from an ideal situation! What kind of terms are you looking at for the new lease? How long will it be for? What is the rate? What is the yearly increase? This is usually based on the national CPI aka Consumer Price Index, but it could be a fixed amount instead. When I had my pizza place I looked at adding a location in another town. This would have been a purchase of an existing business. We were all set to go, except the landlord would not approve the lease takeover. That was because she didn't like the current tenant and

wanted HIM to finish the lease! It was a weird situation, but it happens.

7. What kinds of changes would you want to make to the business? I do not recommend changing major things the business does in the beginning. But, if you are positive it the change will help a bad reputation, then consider making the change. But my point here is that if you have changes in mind, does the current location support those changes? For example, if it is a restaurant that uses electric ovens and you want to change to natural gas. Does natural gas service exist at that location? Those are the types of things you will need to look at.

8. As mentioned in number 7, I do not recommend making abrupt changes to things that already work. Make those changes over time. Let the current customers get used to them so you do not lose them (as an example, give them two choices – the old way and the new way), unless you want to lose them (which is a possibility!). The first thing the new owners did after buying my pizza business was to change the sauce recipe. We had been using that recipe for over 13 years. They lost 25 percent of their business over a short period of time and could not figure out why. I knew what it was that contributed to why. Can you make a good guess?

9. Negotiate everything. Make sure you know whether the inventory is in the price. Most times it is not. In a restaurant, inventory fluctuates, and the current owner wants to get compensated. Same thing with specialty licenses such as liquor or tobacco or firearms licenses. Make sure you know EVERYTHING so there are no surprises if you decide to buy the business.

10. You will need to complete most or all steps from the chapter "Starting Your Business." Even though you are buying an existing business, you will need to register as the new legal owner of it. You need to figure out how you are going to organize the ownership as described in that chapter. So, follow all those steps and do everything you need to do to assure success in your new business!

Branding and Marketing Your Business

Part 1: Branding, Marketing, and Advertising

Branding, marketing, and advertising your business is a huge task. You will want to make progress every single day in this role. Many people think of marketing as advertising – it is – but it is much more than that. Marketing encompasses the entire customer experience. It is what they hear and see about your business on the outside. It is the way your business looks and feels and smells like. It is the type of product and service that people receive on the inside. Everything about your business is your responsibility. Now that you understand that (and hopefully accept it!) we can move on to the nitty gritty.

Let's talk about advertising first since that is what most people consider marketing to be. How will you get the word out that you are in business? Do you sell local products or services? Statewide? Nationwide? All over the world? Consider very carefully how you will advertise the business. Make sure the method of advertising works for your business. Make sure the advertising budget works for your business as well.

Here are many of the methods of advertising. I listed them mostly in order from least expensive to most expensive. The first 3 are excepted because you need these first. This is not an exact science and your business may differ, so don't count on the order too much:

1. Get a logo. You can use a logo designing computer program purchased from an office supply store for about $30. Or, you can have a professional logo created for you for several hundred dollars. But, get a logo – one that does your business justice. If you don't like it right away, you won't like it later. Change it and make it something you do like. The logo doesn't have to be fancy - it can be the company name in a special font, for example. Look at big company logos. Then develop a slogan and integrate that into your logo. Look at both general business slogans and business slogans in your industry to get an idea for a slogan. Then make something up that you like and try it out on your friends. Put your

logo on everything that you print. Put it on your website(s) too. It will tie everything together that you do. Try to make your slogan fit your business name. We were Outlaw Pizza, pizza so good it was outlawed by the competition (true story). Glick's Computer Repair - Help is just a 'Glick' away!

2. Get business cards made, unless you ONLY do business out of state or overseas! Put on the card your name and title. Put the name of your business and what you do. List your primary services and products first if you have a lot. Add your phone number, email address, and if you are a brick and mortar, your physical address. If you do not have a logo (but you should!) you can use a piece of clipart. Your office supply shop or online supplier may have some available, so it dresses up the card a little. Make the business card stand out somehow. Most important, make sure it is readable by everyone. Senior citizens don't want to use a magnifier to read your business card, as an example! Color-blind people need high contrast letters off the background for all signs and print media.

3. BRICK AND MORTAR BUSINESSES: You MUST have a sign for your business. Some of them are quite expensive. But, this will depend on what may or may not be currently in the slot for your space. Every building is different. If you have a very limited amount of space on a post sign, only put your primary form of business

there. Do not worry about the name. Put your name on the pendant sign on the building if you can. People do not need to know the name of your business if they cannot read the sign. What you do is more important. In 1987 my landlord finally sprung for a pole sign in front of our building. We had 4 tenants, so we were very limited to the room we had. Instead of putting Verde Pizzeria and having no one being able to read it, I had it read PIZZA. Business increased immediately. TIP: for goodness sake, please use a high contrast sign!! I am red-green color blind. I can't tell you the number of signs I cannot read the lettering on! The sign creator would use this beautiful plethora of colors in the sign. But, they did not make the letters high-contrast with the background. So I and the other color-blind people in the world cannot read it! How many people is that? Up to 5 percent of males and a very small percentage of females. Guess what? I do not patronize those businesses! I have no clue what they do based on their sign when driving past them at 45 miles an hour.

4. PRIMARILY LOCAL BUSINESSES: Word of mouth. This is where you, your employees, or your customers spread the word about your business. A positive manner is preferable! (See Reputation Management in part 3 of this chapter) This obviously will be more challenging in the beginning. You may not have employees and you may not have customers. This is going to be up to you. I recommend you join a local networking group such as the

chamber of commerce. Go to meetings and spread the word. Talk to people that you see every day. Talk to the grocery store clerk and other people that you see when you are out and about. Give out free samples if you can in exchange for a review. Hand out your business card to everyone that you see. Even to people that may not use your business; they may know someone that will! If you have the margin, get business cards made up that give a discount to products or services and hand them out. Give out both the discount cards and your regular business cards to everyone you see. Ask if they will accept them from you.

5. Social Networking: Here is a short primer on social networking because if you do this yourself, it will be nearly free (however you might want to just hire someone to do it, especially as you get busier).

a. If you are not on Facebook, get yourself a Facebook account. If you do not have an email account get one. Gmail is preferable because you will need to manage your Google Business account. Get Internet if you do not have it! You can get a Gmail email account for free that you can register your Facebook account with. Then make some Facebook friends. You do know some people, right? If you don't, you are very much not in the right career!! Ask them to be friends on Facebook. Then start a fan page for your business – the current web address as of 2018 is www.facebook.com/pages/create.php . Fill out the information as completely as possible for your page. Then like your page – that's very important. Next, invite your Facebook friends and relatives to like your page. Now you have some fans.

b. Add some interesting content to your Facebook fan page. Your new business page is currently called a fan page. Don't know what to post? Use the search bar at the top of the Facebook page to search for other businesses that are like yours. See what they tell their fans. Tell your fans similar information (or other related information) in your own words. Do not just copy and paste. It is also okay to search for the word "memes" on Google. Search with your type of business in the search field (for example "plumbing memes"). Then copy (save to your computer first then upload to Facebook) and post those on your Facebook page. Memes are pictures with sayings on them. They are typically not copyrighted so they are okay to share on your Facebook page. IMPORTANT!!! Do NOT just copy normal pictures off websites and post them on your Facebook page. Do not post them on your website. This could be a copyright violation and a business can sue you for posting it. Bad things could happen. So, don't do it. You can use pictures on your website or Facebook page. You can either take them yourself or buy the rights to use them through a website like shutterstock.com. You own your own image copyrights. Cool, right?

c. Post on your fan page often. Post at least once every few days. Post more often if possible. Post helpful information. Post free recipes, fun things to do, surveys etc related to your business. People love free information – how-to's are a great way to build rapport. People LOVE giveaways! Give away anything that people perceive to be of value. I have had great luck with 10 or 25-dollar Starbucks gift cards.

d. Go to other Facebook fan pages in your city or area and make comments while you are logged in under your fan page. People will see that you are there and that you are friendly and may like your page. Share posts from those entities on your fan page if they are appropriate. Do this every day. At some point you will start to build 'organic' fans, or fans that you get without having to pay for them.

e. After you have a few posts on your fan page, consider promoting some posts through Facebook. You will have the capability to drill down, right to your zip code if you like, exactly who you will advertise to. Make sure the post is positive and appealing to your potential customers. Again, free information is awesome. How to do things, etc. You don't need to give away the house but give something valuable to people in your market. You don't need to spend much - $5 a day is the smallest amount you can spend at this time. Facebook will tell you how many people you will reach for each amount you spend.

f. Get a Twitter, Pinterest, LinkedIn, and Instagram account. But, each successive social networking site takes time to manage. You can share your posts across networks and that does save some time. Consider outsourcing or hiring a social media manager if you think it would benefit your business. You don't want to spend so much time on it that it takes away from the most important aspect of your business – managing it. Do you sell business to business products and services? You will want to take advantage of a LinkedIn account. If you have a sales channel, you can use their Sales Platform.

g. **YOUR PAGE LINK IN EACH SOCIAL ACCOUNT SHOULD END THE SAME!**

Check this out:

- ✓ https://facebook.com/g6webservices
- ✓ https://twitter.com/g6webservices
- ✓ https://linkedin.com/in/g6webservices
- ✓ https://instagram.com/g6webservices
- ✓ https://pinterest.com/g6webservices

Cool, right? Got it?

6. Flyers and Brochures: If your business can use flyers or brochures, I recommend you use them. They provide more information than a business card. They can highlight the strong areas of your business and you can make them different sizes. I also recommend that you have a professional design them for you. This is a part of your marketing and you want to make the best presentation possible. Make sure the information you include will be current for at least a few months. Re-making flyers gets expensive so plan well. Print as many as possible because the per-unit cost goes down for the more that you make. This goes for anything printed.

7. Newspapers and Local Shoppers: Does your local newspaper or local shopper have a good readership? Can you can come up with a strong advertisement? Then this may be a way to go. The only way to tell is by trial and error, unfortunately. I would make a compelling offer that they can only get if the customer either mentions the ad or clips a coupon. This way you will know how you got your new customer. Newspapers have several different rates. The longer of a term you agree to advertise for, the lower the per-ad cost. Most newspapers will design the ad for you and for the most part they are adequate. But I would consider hiring an ad agency to help with this. They may be able to put the message out in a more efficient manner that will draw more

interest for you. Be sure to use your logo in your advertisements. For goodness sake make sure your current contact information is there and it is nice and big, as well. Using ad-spend and not having current contact info in the ad is a complete waste!

8. Telephone Books. These used to be the primary form of advertisement for many businesses. Many businesses were very successful with them. But, the Internet has all but taken over for the place where most people go and search for their needs. I am not saying NOT to advertise in the phone book (as of 2018). But I do recommend you research your options based on your business. If there are other businesses of your type advertising in the phone book, then it may be a place to consider. But if there are none, there is a reason for that. The biggest deterrent to phone book advertising is cost. It is SO expensive to advertise in them, and believe me, bigger ads are not always better in print. It all depends on the ad itself and the readership.

9. Radio and Cable Television: The next place to look to advertise is radio and television. These avenues may or may not be right for your business. If you see or hear your competition advertising on the stations, then it may be right. Radio and Cable Television advertising is a bit complicated. This is because you need to know your target market. You need to know your market's age, income levels, likes and dislikes, etc before you advertise. Advertising on

the wrong station is throwing your money away. I discovered that a lot of people that listen to country radio do not buy pizza in our then local market. But when that local radio station switched to rock and pop, the advertising began paying off. Again, know who you are selling to and what they watch and listen to. Like newspaper advertising, the more ads you sign on for, the less your per-unit cost will be. You can always negotiate, too! As always, make sure your logo displays on all television advertising.

10. **Your Very Own Website:** I recommend a website for almost every single business. Almost everyone is online these days. Most people now use a smartphone for searching. Your website can be useful for one or more things. It can provide information about your business. It can book appointments if you are a service-based business. It can sell products for you, or it can be a hop-off point to another website or even social networking. The easiest but most expensive way to get a website is to hire a web designer. This can cost $300 to many thousands of dollars, depending on the complexity of the site. All web designers are not created equal. Always make sure you get real samples of their work so you can decide if that is the person you want to use. You can also have a funnel site designed to get leads. I use ClickFunnels for this. I have arranged to get you a 14 day free trial – simply head over to my special link at https://clickfunnels.com/?cf_affiliate_id=787294&affiliate_id=787

<u>294</u> . Email me after you sign up and I will provide you with some awesome bonuses along with any support you need!

11. After you decide the purpose of the website, speak with the designer. You want to know that they can do will fit in with your end goal for the site. Make sure the designer feels comfortable with the work. Designers have different knowledge points and you want to verify the one you choose can do the work. Also, you may be able to get the hosting through the web designer. This is something you can also do yourself if you feel comfortable. There are three primary services that you pay for. Domain registration, website hosting, and email hosting. There are others but those are the primary services. Many companies provide packages with one rate for everything. Other companies sell everything ala carte. You pay for each thing. This is usually more expensive than package deals. Either way, compare the designer's rates for what you can get yourself. Make sure it includes email service. Ask the designer that if you and she part company, who will have control of your website. The answer should be you.

12. You can go to a place like ours at https://g6webhost.com and purchase a domain and hosting. It costs $15 a month with the now required (for business) SSL certificate and one email address (upgrade packs are available). The hosting package includes everything you need for your business's website except the website design. Call 800-590-2085 and we will help you through

the entire process. We can also design a website for you. Or if you have a designer give the sign-on credentials to your web designer. They will get your website set up. Ask your web designer to set up email accounts for you as well. Ask how to check that email either through webmail or through a mail client like Outlook.

13. If you are tech-savvy you can create your own website. There are thousands of free WordPress templates available. There are tons of free plugins. These add functionality and responsiveness to your website. Be sure to use a WordPress Firewall to help protect against the bad guys out there. Bad guys deface and hack websites. Google "WordPress Firewall" to see what I am referring to. In any event, you will want your website to look professional. It becomes a natural extension of your business AND has to be useful in what you want it to do (it's purpose).

14. Pay Per Click and other Web Advertising. This can either be super-cheap or super-expensive. It depends on how you set it up and how much of a budget you are looking to spend. This is not a good idea for all businesses. It is something that you want to study before going with pay-per-click. Unfortunately, a lot of businesses spend a lot of money getting clicks. These clicks are from their competitors or "lookie-loos" that do not want to buy from you. Pay-per-click can put you at the top of Google quickly. Although, a paid position not an organic position. The things you see at the top of Google searches include paid search results. Again – this is

trial and error – I recommend that you do not get locked into a long term or high-dollar contract. Test the waters.. if it works, then spend more. If it doesn't then spend your money elsewhere.

15. Magazines: I saved magazines for last. They are generally very expensive to advertise in. You must know your market niche super well. Also, you have to pick the magazine that might give you the most bang for your buck. I have tried magazines for my business and I would think they would have worked but they did not. My advice is to not get locked into a long-term contract if you decide to go this route. You may shoot yourself in the foot if you do.

16. Final Word on Advertising – your advertising is an extension of your business. It is a part of your branding. Do you want people to consider you to be moral, ethical, and honest? Then you must treat your advertising the same way. Do not make hyped claims about how good your business is. If you want to do that, use testimonials instead. This is called Social Proof. Real people sound off about their real experiences with your business. See reputation management in part 3 of this chapter. This will give you more information about reviews and testimonials. Review your commercials or ads before they go live. Make sure you are happy with them. Make sure they are an honest portrayal of your business. They need to portray how you want to be perceived by your current and potential customers. One bad advertisement can

destroy years of goodwill that you have built up. Can you think of an ad that rubbed you the wrong way and ruined the reputation of that business for you?

BUSINESS SECRET OF THE MILLENIUM:

MAKE IT AS EASY AS POSSIBLE TO DO BUSINESS WITH YOU!!

Why? Because customers that have a hard time doing business with you will be a tough sell for repeat business AND they won't give you referrals or great reviews online! What does it mean to make it easy to do business with you? Here are some examples of what you DON'T want:

- They can't reach you when they want to reach you.
- You don't respond to their messages when you say you will
- They must dial down through multiple menu layers on the phone system to get to who they want to talk to or they must wait a long time (even 30 seconds) before they can leave their message.
- Your business is not open when you say you will be or when it is convenient for your customers.
- Finding what they want is more difficult or more time-consuming than what they expect.

- Checkout lines are longer than your customers are willing to wait.
- Your credit card machine takes a long time to process a payment.

TIP: It is the customer's PERCEPTION of these things, not necessarily what ACTUALLY happens!

If these things happen, among a million other things that can go wrong, they will not do business with you. Period. You are in business to fill a need for your customers/clients/patients. You must fill that need BETTER than any of your competitors. By a long shot. If they cannot find you, reach you, talk to you, get the product or service, or pay you, EASILY, they will go somewhere else. They will go to a competitor that does that ONE thing better than you! Consider the following:

1. If you want your customers to find you on the Internet, is your phone number and address (if appropriate) prominently displayed on every page of your website?
2. Is there a contact form that is easily accessible on your website, and is it easy to use? Does it make them fill out a ton of information before they can send the form, or does it only ask for the most pertinent information? (Hint – do not provide your email address on web pages – use a simple contact form instead. Providing your email address will invite spammers and viruses to your email address)

3. Are your hours prominently displayed somewhere on each of your web pages?
4. When people call you, do they have to listen to and drill down through layers of menus before they finally get through to a live person? Or do they get a person after a reasonable amount of time or one or two button pushes?
5. If you are busy on the phone with another customer do you have a voicemail system to leave a message or do the callers get a busy signal? Do you return your voicemails consistently and in a timely manner? **TIP: Do you state in your greeting when the (prospective) customer/client/patient can receive a call back?**
6. Are your store hours posted and easily readable on your storefront? **TIP: If at all possible, your store hours should be readable from a vehicle parked in the parking lot so you do not make people get out of their car (think: weather).** They should also be accurate in your Google Maps listing. We were on vacation recently and wanted to buy our brunch from a very popular bakery. They close when they sell out of baked goods, which is understandable. We pulled into their one-way driveway which is located one building away from their store. We then pulled into their rear parking lot (and only parking lot) about 11:30 am. We got out of the car in the stifling heat and walked to the entrance at the front of the building. They had put up their sign in the front door that said they were sold out. So we walked back to the car in the stifling heat, unfulfilled. My wife looked at

me and said "Couldn't they just place a sign in their parking lot that said this?" Yep, my wife is awesome. Can you learn that one from her?

7. Is your contact number prominently displayed as well so if you are closed they can call and leave a message?
8. Are you actually open during the hours you say you will be, or do you lock the door at random times? One of my friends ran a business this way. He was a great friend, not a great business-person.
9. What other aspects of your business could, or would customers find it easy or difficult to do business with you?
10. Rate your business 1-10 on how easy you feel it is to contact you and do business with you (be honest, the only person you will cheat is yourself!). Where can you improve? Can you implement the changes easily?

Part 2: You have customers/patients/clients! Now what?

You need to understand what your customer sees through their eyes. What do they see when they walk through the door, or contact you by phone (or some other method), or they see you out and about?

Can you see it? Does the customer get a good or bad initial impression? What does your customer get when they contact you by phone? Do they get a friendly and patient voice on your end? Or are they getting someone that is having a bad day and obviously grouchy?

First time customers (and even regulars!) will be sensitive to that so be aware of the customer's experience. The same thing applies to walk-in customers. They can hear AND see you and your employees. Is your and your employees' dress appropriate for your business? Is personal hygiene an issue (or hair length, body piercings, tattoos, etc)?

What else does the customer see, hear, smell, or feel when they walk through the door? Is the place clean (look everywhere, including the ceilings, ceiling fans, vents, corners where the walls meet each other and the floor, baseboards, and ESPECIALLY the rest rooms!)? Is the environment attractive? Is there a stench in the building? Or, does it smell appropriate for the business? I went into a Mexican chain restaurant a long time ago. The stench of old grease was so bad I walked right back out the door? Is the décor appropriate for the business? Is there anything dangerous that could hurt someone? Is the floor slippery (after it rains as an example)? Are the sidewalks icy or stairs slippery? Is it too hot or too cold inside the building?

What is the rest of the experience like? Remember, you are NOT only selling a product or service; you are also selling an experience!

Here are two questions that you need to answer. 1) Is the experience better than your competitor's and 2) IS EVERY EXPERIENCE AS GOOD AS IT CAN GET?

If you sell products, do they please most of your customers? You will NOT EVER make everyone happy so keep that in mind. However, you do want to strive for at least 98% satisfaction or you probably will not stay in business. If you provide a service, are the customers happy with it? Can you do better? Maybe talk more, or talk less? Smile more? Do you empathize with your customers when they have issues (no matter what)? Do your customers feel like they get a good deal from you? Do you make them feel special and appreciated?

It is super important that customers feel welcomed when they patronize you. They also need to feel appreciated when they (or you) leave. Most them want a personal connection to you, like you are their friend. So, give that to them if you can. They will walk away feeling like a million dollars, even if they only spent five with you. My wife always used to tell me that we killed people with friendliness in our restaurant. But that's how we did business and that's one reason we were so successful.

People love being called by their first names. They love knowing that you care enough to know their wife or husband's name. They love knowing you are interested in them. Become personable if you are not, or if you are not one of those that can be find a manager that can. Always thank the customer for coming in, as well. How many times do you go into a fast food place, you place your order, get your food, and you are not thanked for the business? You will almost NEVER get a thank you going out the door of that place. Would it change your opinion of the place if you did? Learn from the things that upset you about going to other businesses. Instill those values in yours. Be PROUD of what you sell and what you do in your business, AND of the service that you provide.

CUSTOMER LOYALTY: A very important aspect of marketing is customer loyalty. How can you keep your customers loyal to you and better yet, how can you get your customers to tell others about you? Most businesses use some type of loyalty program. Buy 10 of this, get that free or use this many of that and get this for half price. Customers love deals and they love to talk about your business if you treat them right. So figure out something you can give away (or discount), and make it a part of a popular item package. My pizza business was called Outlaw Pizza. As a promotion, we gave out an Outlaw Buck with every large or extra-large pizza. The customer saved 10 and handed them in for a free large cheese pizza (toppings extra). People LOVED them! In another business I asked customers to tell their friends or relatives about me. I handed them a flyer at the end of our business together that served as a rebate form. They filled it out and gave it to their friend that had a need for my service. When their friend used my service, the referrer got a rebate and the new customer also got a discount on the service! What did it cost me to do that? It cost a few sheets of paper. It also cost 1 minute of my time to explain what it was and how to use it. It also cost the time and minimal cost to write the rebate check and send it out. I only had to pay for that customer once, but they kept coming back. Definitely a win, and the cost of the new customer was much cheaper than other methods of advertising.

Part 3: Reputation Management

At the end of each transaction your customers, every one of them, will have an opinion of your business. This is not to mention the very first time your customer learns about your business. Some opinions will be stronger than others. Unbelievably, opinions can be VERY strong. They can swing from extremely negative to extremely positive (and anywhere in-between!). Those people will relate their experiences to their friends. They will relate them to their neighbors, relatives, and anyone else that will listen! The Internet is the biggest forum in the world, and there are plenty of places that have ears there. All someone has to do is talk and as long as their opinion is perceived as rational they will be heard. But, it is easy to manage your reputation on the Internet similar as it is for someone to post their opinion about it. So let's get cracking and figure out this reputation management stuff!

To begin, here is the question of The Century. What opinion did my customers get from my business, and how are they going to distribute that opinion, if they do? Most reputation management comes in AFTER they discuss their opinion of your business. This is rather unfortunate, but true. For negative reviews, it is like putting out fires, or if it was positive – great!! You should always respond and thank them for their patronage. Thank them for their lovely review of your business. This shows that you are in-touch with your community AND that you care.

If on the other hand they perceived to have a negative experience with your business, they will not write nice things about it. They may even make things up or stretch the truth. One time I got an Angie's List review from someone that I had done work for. – I completed the job to his satisfaction but something I had said at some point offended him. I may have been busy focusing on the job. I may have explained that I would answer his question afterward or something to that extent. I may have been less friendly in my response than he would have liked. Needless to say, I got the feeling he wasn't happy with that, and he did end up writing me a poor review. He even gave me a C for timeliness, even though I was exactly on time for the appointment! A 'C' – because he was unhappy about whatever it was I said. Nothing I could do about that! People can be vindictive, and they will let the world know about it. Your only defenses are to try and head them off before they happen and to respond when they do.

So, what do you do if you receive a poor review of your business on the Internet? The first thing to know is what kind of reviews you are getting on the Internet! Remember we cannot do anything about that which we are unaware of. Here is a great start – go to Google online. Type the name of your business, the city and/or state you are located in and add the word 'review' to your search term. If there are any reviews online for your business, they should show up there. You can also do the same things for products that you sell or intend to sell. This way you can get a feel for what current users of the product say about it.

Read your reviews with care. You must completely understand every part of it, and NEVER respond to a review the same day you see it. I repeat - NEVER respond to a review the same day you see it. I guarantee that you will be sorry that you did, no matter what the circumstances. If it was a negative review, you may feel very emotional and defensive. It is YOUR business they attacked, and you will not be happy about it. Here is what you will want to do instead: write the response to the review in an email to yourself. Save it as a draft when you are done for the moment.

Write down on paper other ideas you might have for the response as you go through your day. Change your draft response as you see fit. You will even want to wait 2 or 3, or even more days before responding to it. Chances are on the 2nd or 3rd day you will probably throw most of your original response away. Then you will write a new one, especially if your first one was emotional. Also, ask a trusted individual to read your response and provide suggestions. Read how other people have responded to negative reviews online. What was your impression of them? Would you still patronize that business (did you get a positive feeling from the response?) or would you avoid it at all costs? That's what you want to discern against in your response to the review.

Did an employee serviced the customer? Was the review negative? Ask the employee what happened. Try not to shoot first and ask questions later. There are always 2 sides to every story. You will want to ask the employee their side of the story. You do not want them feeling threatened like they will lose their job. Gather all the facts that you can. Then, when you are ready to respond, consider the voice of the customer. How did they feel and why did they feel that way? What if you were in their shoes given the circumstances? Would you feel the same way? When you begin to target your response to them, begin by putting their shoes on your feet. Empathize with their situation (if warranted). Remember that person will not be the only one reading it. Countless other potential customers will as well. We all make mistakes. What those people are looking for is to see if you take responsibility for the mistakes. And whether we are going to learn from them or continue to repeat them. I always told my kids growing up. Yes, you made a mistake. Apologize for it. Then after you apologize say that you will not do it again and make your best effort not to repeat it. Same thing here – that is all that you can do.

The situation is much more difficult if the customer was completely in the wrong. Or, if the 'customer' was not a customer at all and could be a competitor looking to cause trouble for you. If this is the case, say so. Once I received a one-star review on Yelp. The person allegedly called me to confirm an appointment. Not only did I not return the call I also did not bother to show up. I researched my records. I discovered that this person never left me a voicemail as she said she had. I did not even service the area she said she was from at the time! I explained this in my response. I also explained that had this been an actual issue I would have taken responsibility for it.

Local (not online) reputation management will be more difficult to manage. You will may not know who is talking about your business or what they are saying. Your best defense here (and always!) is prevention. Always put your best foot forward and give people what they want and what they deserve to get. Go the extra mile – under-promise and over-deliver. Make them so happy they won't have a choice BUT to be happy! Then, give the customer a way to discuss their opinion of your business. Survey cards are great! You can get their contact information if they leave it. You will also get the review and you will know their real feelings about their experience. Give them a reason to fill out the survey. A dollar off a product can be a great reason to fill out the survey and you will get a higher response that way. Provide the pen and let them take it home! Remember – make it EASY!! I guarantee you will get responses you will be proud of, and some that will really surprise you.

As you can see, there are many aspects to reputation management. Not everyone is going to be happy with our efforts in business. Your best defense, and offense, is to:

1) mitigate ANY issues in the business by using the advice from this book
2) take responsibility for everything that happens in your business
3) assure your current and potential customers that you will make an occasional mistake. You will take responsibility for it. You will do everything in your power to make it right for the customer that was on the receiving end of that mistake. You will do everything you can to learn from that mistake, so it does not get repeated.

Well, yes, that may not happen, but at least that's the attitude you want to take. Murphy's Law strikes hard sometimes. No matter how few times you make mistakes, the same mistake might happen to the same customer! No matter how hard you try!! We took pride in the pizza business that our pizza toppings were accurate. We gave the customer only what the customer wanted. Sometimes we would forget to leave off the bell peppers or onions on our combination pizzas if that was requested. We could make 1000 deluxe pizzas and one or two of them would have that issue. Wouldn't you know it? It would happen to the same customer – on multiple occasions! Yes; Murphy's Law. Ick.

How to get more reviews. You do know that the only way to combat most negative reviews, is to get more and better reviews, right? So how do you go about getting more reviews? Good question….. Some platforms are different than others in the way you go about getting them. Yelp, for example, FROWNS completely on merchants asking for reviews. Dumb policy, right? Well they do have their reasons, and here it is. They feel that you will only ask people to leave you a review when they will leave a positive review. Yep - duh. Of course, that will happen!! They don't want to upset the balance of initiative. Never-mind that people are more inclined to leave reviews when they are unhappy about an experience. This happens more often than when they are happy about an experience.

How in the world do they know when you asked? They have a very sophisticated algorithm. It does a very good job (but not perfect) of choosing reviews that are too positive for example. Also, reviews that are not descriptive enough, or when the reviewer only has one or two reviews that they have given from that profile. Yelp then can deem it to be unreliable and send it to the "Not Recommended Reviews" section. Sometimes reviews can be removed completely for violation of their TOS (Terms of Service). They will remove them for any reason they wish. They will not offer an explanation, primarily because their bot does those things. No human even touched it so no one can explain what it was that caused the problem.

Okay you might be saying, that's great info. But how do you get people to leave you a review on Yelp???? The ONLY thing you can do (as of 2018) is to 'proudly' display the Yelp member poster in your window. Yep - that's it. I suppose for home-based service businesses you could also 'proudly' tell your customers while onsite that you are a Yelp member. Other than that, there are no ways to do it (according to Yelp TOS) so don't even try. Remember of course to always respond to Yelp reviews. Keep in mind that the reviewer will receive all your responses through email. You can start a conversation with them. But I recommend that all conversations be held offline, as I suggested earlier.

In regard to Google (and other platforms), right now it is easier to get reviews on them. One tactic that I recommend to all business owners is to ask all customers/clients/patients a simple question. "Is there any reason why you wouldn't give us 5 stars on Google based on your experience today?" (Or choose whatever platform you use) Saying this puts the bug in their head to do this for you. It also calls out any negativity that they experienced so you can address it immediately. You do not have to wait to see that negative review online! Do EVERYTHING you can to address ANY negative comments immediately. This way your customer comes back to do business with you. He or she will also relay the experience to their friends, relatives, and social media. They will explain how something went wrong. And that you cared enough to fix the problem immediately and to their satisfaction! Most people understand that things go wrong. What they will NOT tolerate though is not addressing or taking responsibility for those issues. You MUST do that, or you will lose more business in less time than anything you could possibly think of.

Part 4: Marketing Summary

Marketing is everything current or potential customers experiences regarding your business. From your advertising to your signage. From how dirty or clean your business is to the reviews on the Internet or what they hear from others. From the experience in the business itself to anything else in regard to your business. It is true, you do not always have control over everything. But, you will want to be certain that everything that is in your control is positive. It must be positive for ALL current and potential customers/clients/patients. You have control over how your employees answer the phone. You have control over how you greet the customer face to face. You have control over the quality of your resold products to the extent that you decide what and what not to sell. If you are the manufacturer, you have direct control over your products. You decide what suppliers to use. If you get a poor product from one supplier, move to another. One example of that is a restaurant. You have control over how clean your store is. You have control over what kind of advertising you do. Take the time to look at the big picture. Ask your customers about their experiences. Always look for ways to make your business better for customers. In small business, complacency is your enemy; positive innovation is your friend.

Here is another huge epiphany that you probably knew. You may not have thought much about it. **All the advertising in the world will not bring people to call or in the door if your reputation is poor, especially your online reputation compared to your competitors (local word of mouth reputation is extremely difficult to monitor and control).** If you have issues with quality, service, or cleanliness, word will get around. You can't change that. All you can change is what is within your control. Don't sell anything you aren't proud to sell. Always make sure your store is clean.

When I was in the restaurant business, if I had a bunch of complaints about something that I was making we changed it to make it better. If I wasn't proud to sell it, I didn't. Same thing in my computer business - I HATE it when stuff doesn't work right! If I was selling something that didn't work properly as it should or failed quickly, I changed or stopped selling it!

If you are having quality issues, you need to determine what's going wrong and fix it - fast. If you can't fix it, take the product off the market until the quality issues get fixed. If you are having service issues -

same thing - figure out what's wrong - fast - and fix it. Same thing with cleanliness - people DO look and people DO care! I can't tell you how many restaurants I go to and the restrooms look like a bomb hit them. The entire restaurant is immaculate, but the restroom looks like S**T.

Go through ALL your stuff that customers see, hear, smell, taste, and touch like a Martian and fix what's not right! Do that at LEAST once a week so you don't get behind and you don't lose touch. Consider hiring 'mystery' shoppers when you are not able to be there. Video cameras are okay, but they don't tell the whole story. You need the whole story.

Wearing Your 'Hats'

Small business owners wear many hats. You wear the owner's hat to bookkeeper to janitor. From chief cook and bottle washer to manager. From hourly employee to marketing exec to advertising exec, and many more. We are not going to be successful unless we do wear all those hats. Ultimately, even if we find someone that can help us, the owner is the one responsible for all decisions. The owner takes responsibility for everything that happens in the business. It is very important that you know yourself and your strengths and weaknesses. If you are not good with money you will want to hire someone that can help you in that area.

The interesting thing about these hats is that one minute you are wearing one hat, and the next minute (or the next second!) you are wearing a different hat. It can make your head spin! The trick here is – just let it flow and don't worry or think about it. You just do what you need to do. This is where those time management techniques will really come into good use – see that chapter in this book.

Here is a list of different hats you may need to wear:
- Owner
- Manager
- Negotiator
- Stocker
- Graphic designer
- Web designer
- Technician
- Merchandiser
- Inventory manager
- Order manager
- Customer service rep
- Order taker
- Salesperson
- Chef
- Cook
- Dishwasher
- Janitor

- Marketer
- Advertiser
- Printer
- Mechanic
- Plumber
- Repairperson
- Bookkeeper

Crazy, right? This probably is not even close to the number of hats you may need to wear over the course of the time in your business!

You need help – when you can afford it! For example, a good accountant or bookkeeper can help a lot. Tons of small businesses fail due to mismanagement of money! You could be bringing in tons of sales and making a huge profit. But if the money isn't there to pay the bills the business will fail. That is a certainty. Businesses need cash to survive. Businesses that stock product or rely on equipment must have ample cash on hand.

How else do you decide which hats you should wear and which ones you should delegate? First, you will want to take a personal inventory of yourself in relation to the needs of your business. What are you good at? What are you not so good at? What do you like to do and what do you not like to do? Those questions are the ones you need to answer to help you figure out where you will need the help.

When I first got into the pizza business, I knew nothing about making pizza. The previous owner trained me for a few hours over the course of two weeks. But I didn't feel confident enough to do it myself. There was a lot to it because it was all homemade! We had to make the dough and the sauce. They had to come out right or they didn't taste good. And of course, there was the actual act of making and baking the pizzas themselves!

I liked to cook, but this was nothing like I had ever experienced. Fortunately (kind of) the previous cook stayed with me for a bit. I don't recommend doing this by the way unless you have built a relationship with them which in this case I had not. So, it was a good thing in this case because I did not have to make the pizzas. Well, it was that way for about three weeks. Then he quit. Yeah, he and I didn't get along too well. He didn't like the new way I did business. So, I threw myself into the fire and had to figure out the pizza business after all. Oh, and one more thing – he decided to get a bit vindictive and added a whole ton of salt to the last batch of sauce he made. Funny the things we remember for decades. Anyway, lesson learned. Always know how to do what your employees do. Know it even better, know how to do it better because you could be the person training the next one, if you aren't already.

Finally, you can move 'out' of hats when you can afford to find and hire people to replace YOU wearing those hats. Do that as soon as you can. Owner burnout is not a fun thing to cope with, and you must work to prevent it. See the chapter on Owner Burnout later in this book.

Employees - You Need Them to Make the Big Bucks

You can't live with them and - well you know the rest. :) You **can** live with them - if they are right for you and you establish a good relationship with them! You need employees if you find that you are not able to run the business by yourself. You might be so busy that you are turning down customers. That is a good situation, but not a good situation to be in. You need employees if your service levels are plummeting. You need employees if you have so many positions to run that you cannot fill them all yourself.

I am not going to lie. This is a huge undertaking because you need to know A LOT about taking on employees. I will do my best to provide you with as much information as I can in this writing. But I will also say that you will need to do your own research on employee hiring in your jurisdiction. You want to make sure you have all your bases covered. You do not want legal issues creeping out from the woodwork. It is enough of a struggle on your own just running your business! Employees can be your biggest asset, or the biggest pain in your rear. I hope this chapter will help steer you into the former and not the latter!

My former employer at Burger King had a saying about employees – he would always say "they come, and they go." That seems like a simple statement. But, it is multi-dimensional from a business owner's standpoint. We must expect that we will hire employees. At some point – it could be the next day, or years down the road, that person will leave, or you will be forced to let them go. They always go - then the cycle starts again.

You will be the one to decide if you need employees. You will decide what roles they will fill and how many you will need. You will decide on the hiring and firing of those employees, among other things. You need to understand all federal and state laws in regard to hiring and firing of employees. You will also need to make sure you are in compliance with all laws involving employees. You will want to check all federal, local, and state laws as they apply to you regarding minor hiring. You need to know about tobacco, liquor, and firearms sales if they apply to you. You also need to understand and be OSHA compliant (if this applies to you). You need to understand HIPAA compliance (in healthcare) and wage laws. That's only a start! You may also be a required to hang certain posters for your employees in your establishment. You will want to research that as well.

You will need to comply with state, local, and federal tax authorities. Contacting a reputable accountant will be to your advantage. You need to know what to withhold from employee's paychecks. You need to know when that money payment is due. You also need to send along any money that your business must pay for the employee's welfare. Examples include Social Security, Medicare, and unemployment insurance. Workers' Compensation insurance protects employees in cases of injury. You may need that, depending on your circumstances. Contact your state authorities to help you determine if and how much you need.

You need to have accurate job descriptions available for each position. When you proceed to hire someone, you can provide that description in the job listing and as a part of the training. You may also want to have an employee handbook available. Employees will need a reference of what you expect from them and what they can expect from you. It is like a contract, and it is always good to spell things out. Communication is going to be key in your quest for successful employer-employee relations.

We have gotten the legal stuff out of the way. Let's go through the process of hiring, training, managing, and terminating employees. I am telling you this before we even start. The mere fact that you have employees will be the most frustrating and yet at other times the most rewarding part of being in business. Keep that in mind as you go through the never-ending process!

HIRING EMPLOYEES: Hiring employees is one of those things that you have to go through – it is a process. If it makes you feel any better, the process is no more fun for the prospective employee than it is for the employer. Don't put an ad in the paper, a Help Wanted sign in the window, or an advertisement on the Internet yet. First, you need to know exactly what it is that you are hiring for. You need the job title and the job description. Come up with the pay grade (low pay to high pay for the position) and benefits package if any (or none). Determine any other pertinent information you will want the prospect to have. If you already have that then great! You are ready to advertise the position. The last question is this: do you want people to fill out your proprietary application or only send in a resume? In filling out your application you will be able to ask them specific information. That is information that you may not get from a resume. So this may be an avenue you wish to explore. Know what questions you cannot ask by law both in the application and in the interview.

Where to advertise your position? If you have a storefront, a Help Wanted sign could work (except if you are a restaurant – don't use that – it makes you look bad). Put an ad in the local paper either in the paper itself or online or contact your local employment office. If you need temporary help, see if there is a temporary employment service in your area.

One of my first jobs in the 1979 recession was with a temp labor company called Manpower. It's a great organization and they screen candidates for you. There is also no payroll tax because they take care of all that for you. You set the pay grade and they bill you for everything in the package including the taxes and their fee. Yes, it is rather expensive. You wouldn't want to find full time permanent workers there but in a pinch for temporary help it works great. There are other temporary employment agencies. Make sure you understand completely how they work - you don't want any surprises.

Other places to look for help include the Internet. You can find all kinds of employment websites. Some of them are more advertising based and pretty much spam everyone. I will not name names, but several free ones come to mind. Others are fee based but do what they say they will do. They do not spam your inbox everyday with junk mail offers. I recently placed a job offer on Indeed and got good results. Jobbing.com is another fee-based employment website. But the last time I looked they were very expensive to advertise in. Check them out anyway – they may have become more reasonable with their rates. Craigslist is another venue to place an employment ad and it is cheap, and you may have great results. There are always tons of people looking so make your job description as specific as possible.

Don't be afraid, in the job description, to state exactly what you need and don't need, from your employees. If you need them to have a valid driver's license and a clean driving record in the last two years, then say that. If they need to be clean-cut then say that. You cannot discriminate based on any of your federal, state, or local laws so make sure you look at them. The more descriptive you are in your ad, the more qualified the candidate resumes you will receive. I also include one more thing in my ad. I tell the readers NOT to respond if they don't fit the qualities required for the position. I tell them not to waste my time or theirs. It helps! One more thing. Make them respond via email with a resume. Or if you are brave, put an online application and have them download it and fill it out, and return it in person. I say if you are brave because then they will know what place it is and you will start getting phone calls. That's one thing I advise against. You don't need 100 phone calls coming in while you are trying to run your place, asking about the position.

I also recommend against putting "Help Wanted" signs in the door. One of my friends told me that many years ago and never, ever put one up in my door or windows. Many restaurants go through help quickly. If they put the sign up every time they need help it makes them look like they go through employees. Which may indeed be the case, but you still don't need that kind of public exposure. Keep it a 'secret' when you need help. Hire in private. You will not get as many applicants, but your business will have a more favorable public opinion.

Now you have begun to receive applications and resumes. You will want to weed through them and pick out the best of the best. Remember this: people will lie. Not all people, but some, and many will bend the facts in their favor. You will need to be able to recognize those lies and fact bends. Yes, the lies may get them an interview, but you will need to flush them out. Look at their previous job experience - was it in line with the job position you need? Did they quit after a very short time? Do they have a history of quitting after a very short time (never a good sign)? Were there gaps in their employment timeline? If so, why? I never said this would be easy! In any event, pick out 5-10 of the best resumes and applications you receive, and call or email them.

Ask to set a time for a phone interview. The purpose of that is to verify their information. You will also ask about any discrepancies in the application. Then drill down a bit further in their knowledge and experience. Ask if you can check their personal and professional references. Any time a person puts "Personal" for a reason for leaving a job, ask them about it. If they badmouth their former employer, they will do that to you as well one day. Probably best to stay clear of that person, even if they are a great prospect. But if they say it didn't work out or they didn't get along with the boss then they may be okay to look at. That happens to everyone at one time or another. After the phone interviews, you should be able to rule out all but 3 or 4 of your best candidates. Call all their references and ask if they are re-hirable. Also ask about anything else they might be willing to talk about. You have a very limited scope of questions that you can ask former employers (like you can't ask "did they steal from you?"). If all goes well with the references, you will want to call the candidates in for an interview.

    For the interview, you will want to make them feel comfortable. The majority of people will be nervous anyway but do your best to be personable. They are scoping you out as well and they want to work for a nice person, not someone that is mean. I would recommend that you research interviewing job prospects books. There is a lot of psychology that goes into a job interview. You want to do your best to make sure you are hiring the best candidate for the position. You don't want to hire a person, spend all that time and money training them, and then they decide they don't like the job (or you!) and leave. You want to do your best to avoid that scenario. It still might happen, after you cross your t's and dot your I's. But do your best to do your research to limit the possibility.

    During the interview, you will be looking at their personality. Look at their physical characteristics to make sure they are a fit for your position. Notice their body language. Sitting forward means they have interest. Sitting back means they are relaxed and may mean dis-interest as examples. Look for any other signs that may or may not fit the position you are hiring for. Is the person like-able? Are you hiring for a front-facing position? If so, you want them to be friendly. Try to keep the interview to 15-30 minutes at most. Any longer and you will bore the candidate and you may not get any more information anyway.

Ask questions that are pertinent to the position. Ask questions about previous experience. You are not allowed to ask personal questions, even their age, as of current law. But that could change. You may ask them if they are old enough to serve alcohol if that is pertinent to the position. You will need to see their ID to prove it. Try to get a feel to see if that person would be a good fit but eliminate any personal bias (positive or negative). You are looking to fill a job, not make a friend. Speaking of, do your best to never make friends with your employees. It is okay to occasionally socialize with them (in a group is best). You may also wish to have a Christmas party. You need to keep the relationship on a professional level. People will be people and can and will take advantage of that personal relationship. That will not be pretty for you, the employee, or others that work for you. It doesn't matter that you are the owner...promise. Break this rule at your own risk :-)

At the end of the interview always thank the candidate for coming and tell them when you will be in touch. It is good business to always call candidates after the interview. You need to let them know if they got the position – never leave someone hanging. Choosing the best candidate for the job may not be easy. You may have a couple or a few that all have what it takes. You need to pick the best of the bunch, or you may have no one that comes close to having what it takes. Then you will need to decide whether to hold off and interview some more people. Or, you may have to choose someone that may not have it yet but shows potential. REALLY IMPORTANT: If a candidate does not respond fast enough, or something else doesn't go right you can choose to let it slide. But, I would suggest you do not as it is a sign of trouble later. Also, you will want to make sure it is legal for them to work for you. Check all your local and national laws and verify their eligibility.

HIRING: Now that you have selected your winning candidate, give them a call and give them the good news. You will need to have the starting salary in mind, and you will want to ask if they will accept the position. If they do not, find out why. You may be able to work around their reasoning if you set it in your heart that you want that person to work for you. If they do accept, set the starting date and time. Tell the new employee to come with a smile on their face and to be prepared for their new position. Provide any training materials if they need them. Make sure they understand what you expect for their first day and beyond.

TRAINING: Now that you have hired your employee(s), you will need to train them. There is almost always an employee orientation to begin with. This is where you have them fill out necessary legal paperwork and give them a tour of your facility. You can also show them what you do that could help them understand their job. You will talk to them to build rapport and get to know them better. Providing an employee handbook is extremely helpful. It sets expectations of what and what not to do. You will also want to provide an accurate job description in the handbook if possible. Protect yourself. Have them sign a piece of paper that states they received the handbook and will obey all regulations. The orientation process lasts for as long as you say it does – there is no set amount of time for it. After the orientation you will want to get down to business and train your employee for their job.

Having someone train the new employee that has already performed their job functions is ideal. It will save you tons of time training. The trainer can also provide the little tips and tricks that it takes to perform the job better. The trainer can also help the new employee work more efficiently. If you do not have a trainer then you will be the one to train them. You should know what the job entails and your vision of the position. If you do not have a job description for the position, now is a great time to make it – while you are training someone for it. Make modifications to the description as you see fit. Don't feel like it is a one size fits all or it cannot be modified as it can be.

In training, you will want to use the four-step procedure outlined here:

1. Explain what the person will be doing – explain it thoroughly and as clear as possible. If it is a very long explanation, then you will want to break it down into bite-sized pieces. Provide the general overview first. Then go through each step as they understand the previous one.
2. Show the person how to do what they will be doing. Make sure that you explain as you go, and for sure make sure that you do it exactly as you want the employee to do it. Explain yourself if there is any variation at all in what you are doing versus what you expect.
3. Let the employee do it. This is very important. The employee must feel confident in their abilities during training. They must prove they can perform the tasks while you (or the trainer) are watching.
4. Finally, follow up on the training at certain intervals to make sure the employee is doing the job right. Also verify they are comfortable with the procedures. Answer any questions they have. Follow up immediately after a certain period of time. Then follow up repeatedly after specified periods of time. The periods of time will be based on the tasks themselves. Some tasks will need to be followed up on immediately. Then again after 5 minutes, then 15, etc, whereas other tasks may need to be followed up on after a few hours, then a few days. It all depends on the complexity of the task and other factors.

PAYING EMPLOYEES. When I first got into the restaurant business there were no personal computers. Payroll services were beyond my financial capabilities. So, my employees kept track of their time by hand. They wrote the times they worked on a 3x5 card to the nearest 15-minute period, so it was easier to figure out what I owed them. I wrote out every paycheck by hand. I had to look at the payroll tables to determine how much taxes to take out and write the checks by hand. Let me tell you - doing it by hand is not recommended. Get a time-clock or better yet a program on the computer for them to clock in and clock out. The computer program will add up their time for you. If you use a program that can do it - it will even figure out how much the checks should be cut for. The most efficient way to do this entire process is to use a program – one program for all of it! It can keep track of the time, print out the checks AND tell you what you owe in payroll taxes at the end of each quarter. It will also tell you how to pay those taxes. The requirements can be different depending on what you owe and what state you do business in.

Pay your employees on time - without fail. If you are hurting for the money, explain to them WHEN they will get paid and the REASON for the delay. Then do your best to make sure it won't happen again. Your employees, if you have them, are the lifeblood of your business. You don't want your employees gossiping about how you couldn't afford to pay them. That is very bad for business. You also want them to remain loyal and not go job-hunting. Fearing for their job is a scary situation - financial security is very important to them.

Try not to get into the position where you can't afford to pay your help to begin with. Cut down your workforce if you must. Find other ways to cut costs without affecting the quality of your products or services. Look for other things that do not affect customer experiences. Being down and out financially is a horrible place to be - I have been there, and plenty of times. Remember this - when there are good times, bad times will come - we just don't know when. And when there are bad times, good times will come - we just don't know when. It is a fact of life and a circle. Planning AND always having a Plan B are the keys.

EMPLOYEE REVIEWS: In your employee handbook (you DO have one, right?) you should detail your employee review policy. Most of the time a company will review their employee's performance after say 30 days after employment, then after 6 months, then yearly after that, IF the employee makes it that long. Your employee reviews should be in-depth and in-line with their job descriptions. You of course always want your employees to go above and beyond so you should make that clear when you hire them, that you have high expectations and that you want them to consider how they can go above and beyond making contributions to your company's success in their day-to-day jobs.

Make sure that your employee review procedure is formalized. In other words, it should be either in the computer or on paper, and you should have your employees sign them acknowledging their receipt and suggestions for improvement. You don't want the review process to just be a way to slam the employees. The review process should use the sandwich technique (just like in your day to day employee management efforts) - give them good news, then some bad news, then some more good news. You want to make them feel like they are a valuable asset, not a piece of meat. If you can't find good things to say about one of them, perhaps that employee should no longer be working for you?

Just like you count on your employees to do a good job, make sure you are available for them in the review process and in the day-to-day operations if they need you. Perform your evaluations on-time, and verify the employees know the rewards they could be entitled to if they have an excellent review. Great bonuses would include gift cards to places like Starbucks or other fine places to eat or purchase goods, money bonuses, and raises all show appreciation for a job well done. Don't give little quarter raises - make them meaningful so you are appreciated and show appreciation. Make it a win-win for you and for them. They will feel more motivated to help you if you show your appreciation in a meaningful way.

BE SENSITIVE to your employee's needs and emotions. You can tell if someone is having a bad day and if you cannot, then you should work on empathy techniques so you can see these things. If you see that someone is not feeling well physically or emotionally ask them if there is anything you can do. Find ways to interrupt their mood and try to make it better if you can. Compliments can go a long way to making someone that feels horrible to really improving their day. There are all kinds of cool management techniques you can learn - but you must want to learn.

EMPLOYEE PROMOTIONS: Nothing shows an employee that you value them more than a promotion. I always tried to promote from within unless I did not have a capable candidate. Promoting employees is a process. They need to know that you are looking for a position to be filled. They need to be aware of the roles and responsibilities that position holds. I always believed in providing all the information without holding anything back. I felt this method provided the best chances for a successful promotion. If a person was leaving a position, I would look for a good candidate to fill it. I would have the candidate shadow the position for a while during slack times so he or she could feel the position. Then I would have the person fill the role for short periods of time. The current person would supervise and provide feedback. This helps to see if the candidate felt comfortable in the position. It also gives them more information for the position and allows them to ask good questions.

You of course only want to give promotions to those that actually deserve it. Promoting someone does require buy-in from other employees. It is a psychological thing. Employees that feel they qualified but were not promoted may become resentful. This could make life very difficult for the employee, you, and the company in general. This is not a good thing. You must mitigate this problem by getting the buy-in before announcing the promotion. You need to be tactful in getting the buy-in. Feel out the doubts and fears of the people you are announcing to. Sometimes conversations need to be private about these issues. especially if you sense the conversation could turn destructive. You almost need to be a good psychologist sometimes when handling employees. Well-handled situations will be very rewarding to your company. It is a learning experience so be certain to learn from mistakes. They can be very costly.

Your candidate may feel insecure in their new position at first. Make sure you treat them like they are a brand-new employee in regard to feedback. All training and review suggestions as above should come into play. For the first 30 days or so you should discover how the other employees are interacting with the newly promoted employee. Listen for any issues that might be going on which could cause you grief later, even in the short term.

EMPLOYEE DISPUTES: These come in two versions. First, employee disputes with another or more than one other employee. The other comes in the form of a dispute with you. The former can be easier to handle. You probably would not be (but not always) personally involved. The latter can be much more difficult to resolve.

Employee disputes among each other. First, you need to always have a good ear that is listening to potential issues on the job. One of the worst things that could ever happen is to become blindsided. A problem that you should have known that was brewing but you ignored it or chose not to listen is big trouble. Second, when you do notice that there is an issue between two or more employees, act. As soon as you can see that they are not coming to a speedy resolution, get involved and resolve the issues. You don't need them festering in the workplace because they can affect everyone. Productivity will decline and attitudes will degrade if they become out of control.

Here is the way that I handled these issues to resolution…. Have a conversation in private with each employee on each side. Get the best handle you can on the issue(s) at hand. Find out what each side wants so the issues can resolve. Don't let BS cloud the issues. Make sure you find the underlying cause of the problems. Give each side one and only one chance to speak their peace. Take notes during these conversations. Better yet use a smartphone's voice recorder software to record the conversations. Get the participant's knowledge and consent. Get the best grip you can by asking clarifying questions during each interview.

Say all interviews took place you do not feel that you can come to an agreement. Let a trusted individual (or more than one) listen to the conversations. See if they can help you make sense of the issues at hand. Make sure you have a good grip on the situations. Then come to a place where you feel that you can have all parties compromise or at least make peace. Get them together with the key focus of resolving the issues. Make it known that not everyone will get their way completely (and unreasonable requests will not get their way at all!). Tell the parties that you have listened to both sides and the resolution will be what you have decided. You are the boss and the decision maker. What you say goes. But, in your mind you will still feel out the parties. Sometimes we are not confident that our decision is the right one. You can now determine if you came to a satisfactory resolution. If it looks like you did, then you are in great shape. If you did not, then you may have to make some concessions IF one of the parties cannot live with the decision.

You always have the possibility of termination if the situations are not resolvable. The focus should be on the workplace vitality and how it will be affected. You always hope that it will not come down to that, but in some cases it may. No one can predict exactly how people will react to situations presented to them. But if you are fair and they are reasonable people (some are not!) then you will be in a good position and your business can move on unscathed.

Disputes involving you. This is a much more difficult situation. You will be involved which will limit your ability to be objective. Also, because the person you have the dispute with will also feel challenged by your position. You know in your heart whether you can be reasonable in the situation. If you can't be reasonable it will be even more difficult. You could end up without that person working for you anymore. You could end up in court, or a combination of both. It IS EXTREMELY important that you do some soul searching and determine how important this is to you. Do your best to keep the lines of communication open between you. Do your best to come to a resolution that is satisfactory to both of you.

If the employee violated you in some way and you are in the right, then this is an easy decision. if you did not violate the employee in any way AND you have legitimate proof of the wrongdoing. But, if you did violate the employee in some way then you could very well be in a sticky situation. Number One Rule with Employees: always be aware of what you are saying AND doing in with and in front of employees. I always had a policy that I would never regret anything I ever said or did in my business. You should consider the same. I have known business owners that got themselves in trouble with employees. They spent years fighting it off. It's not worth the risks or years of headaches and loss of sleep.

Getting back to the topic at hand. If you are in a dispute with an employee and you find yourself in a difficult situation, you may wish to consider hiring a lawyer. You will need one that specializes in workplace legal issues. This is not something that you want to mess with - your business is much too important. Seek legal counsel if you need it in these situations. But above all, always do your best to be reasonable in dispute situations. Being unreasonable will not contribute to positive relations or positive outcomes.

This is one of the dumbest things I ever did as an employee. I unintentionally got in the middle of a dispute between my boss AND a friend that was also an employee - at the same time! There was a legal dispute between the two of them, and I had to make a statement about how one was treating the other. Each asked me to make the statement. As I look back at this, neither should have asked me to make the statement. I had loyalties to both and both knew it. I felt like if I didn't say yes to my boss I would have lost my job. And if I didn't say yes to my friend I would have lost the friendship. What's an employee/friend to do? Make both statements - and that didn't work out too well either. I didn't lose my job or my friend, but I did hear about it from both! Thought question - what would you have done?

TERMINATING EMPLOYEES: At some time when you have employees you will need to terminate one of them. Terminating employees in one word, sucks. I almost always felt bad having to let them go. I always preferred to lose them to attrition. I never owned a business where there were huge advancement opportunities. We could only have one GM for example in the restaurant. So, like my old boss used to say about employees, "They come and they go." That is the absolute truth. We don't know when that occurs, and when they do go, replacing them can be a great challenge.

There is only one time when I almost enjoyed terminating an employee. That was when this one gal lied, cheated, and stole from me, PLUS had an attitude like she was the Queen Bee. I finally had enough...gave her the money owed to her for that week and told her to get out and never come back. I didn't cuss at her or call her names. She knew what she did, and I knew what she did, and that was enough. So, you see there are times when it people deserve it. But I still felt bad.

There will be two reasons you will generally let an employee go. One of them will be that you don't have enough money to pay for their position anymore (a lay-off). The other will be under the guise of 'poor work performance'. This means almost anything from poor attitude, or any other work performance reason. Theft is also included in that category. But, you never want to make that accusation without solid support.

Let's discuss not having enough money to pay for the position. Make damn sure that you are in that position. Verify that you have the tasks for that position covered before making the final determination. Yes, you will most likely feel bad for the person, and there are ways to help soften the blow. The employee may be able to fill another position that pays less. You could cut down to part-time if you are going through a set-back that you can see will not be permanent. You can also help your employee file for unemployment insurance. That will help cover some of the income shortfall. You may have some contacts looking for help that may be able to use your employee's skills in their business.

There are a lot of factors that you will take into consideration when you need to shrink your workforce. Each individual business's needs will vary, depending on the circumstances. As I have stated several times in this book, running a business is a challenge. All decisions are yours and yours alone, right or wrong in the eyes of the bearer. In regard to this, I only provide general advice here. I may be able to point things out that will assist you in making the decisions that you will need to make.

Lastly and as stated above, you need to have solid proof to terminate someone for theft. Therefore, it is best to find other reasons unless you have that proof. If you have it, then let the person go. Be ready for a fight in case it happens, and make sure you have the evidence you need. As I was finishing the main draft of this book I read the story of a Chipotle employee that was fired for stealing some 600 dollars. The employee sued the company for wrongful termination and won. The award was the cool sum of 8 MILLION dollars. Yes - be super careful about this one.

Restaurants: Risks and Rewards

You have probably heard this before. Restaurants are THE most difficult businesses to run. They have the highest failure rate and the highest employee turnover. BUT they also are the MOST fun to run (if you love them). They also have a HUGE return on investment when run properly. I ran two restaurants at the same time in 1991 - and I will tell the stories - right here.

My first restaurant was a pizza place in a small town in Arizona. The restaurant was opened by a young man and his dad in March 1980. The family had another pizza place about 60 miles away, but the family had split up. The father and son decided to open the satellite operation during the separation. They were not overly successful in the 1.5 years they were there. This was primarily due to the recession and that it was a very small town at the time. Plus, the building was set back from the road and there was no pole sign (believe it or not!). After that time, the family got back together. They were then looking to sell the satellite. I was looking to buy a restaurant. I was about to turn 21 years old.

My dad and I looked at the satellite location. We drove to the business and had some lunch. We noticed everything that we could about the business. We discussed it afterward and decided that it would be a big challenge. An employee and his wife were running the place into the ground using artificial cheese for the pizza. They pre-cooked nearly everything. They also stuck a pool table in the middle of the very small dining area. Even though all those issues existed I felt that I could figure it out. Well figuring it out did happen. It just took another year and three quarters. During that time there was very little business. I got behind on bills, but I literally learned my way through it, eventually.

I learned a ton about running a restaurant in a very short time. If I hadn't, the restaurant would have failed. Failure was not an option for me. What qualified me to run a restaurant? Experience at 3 Burger Kings, the last one as an assistant manager for 1 year. Some experience managing a convenience store, and some classes at the local college. Okay, not a lot really. But I wanted to do it and so I did. One of the first things I learned about was food cost. I learned that everything counts, even the salt and pepper on the tables. Because if you don't count everything, you do not get accurate figures. **TIP: You need accurate figures in business. Without them, you don't know where you are, where you have been, or where you are going.**

The second thing I learned was to listen to customers. Not the one that does nothing but complain about everything. Well yes, okay - listen to them too. :) But when you have several people telling you the same thing, you need to consider changing whatever it is. One thing that Burger King really impressed upon me was the QSC model. If you own a restaurant you know (or should know!) what that stands for. It stands for Quality, Service, and Cleanliness. If you don't observe that model in a restaurant, you won't succeed.

Quality - everything must be the best it can be, always. If you wouldn't eat it then don't sell it. I don't mean that if you don't like bell peppers that you wouldn't sell bell peppers. I mean that if the quality you are selling doesn't work for you then don't sell it. If you aren't proud to sell it then don't sell it. Don't get me wrong - things do go wrong. But….if you have control over it then do something about it. If the steak got burned on the outside (yes it stinks because they are not cheap!), don't serve it. Take it home, give it to the homeless, or do something else with it. Don't hide it by turning it over so the good side is up (this has actually happened to me as a customer!). It does not matter how much it cost you. Seriously. Is that customer's future business and your reputation worth the wholesale cost of that steak? You bet it is. If you disagree, you need to get out of the business. Like yesterday.

Homemade food can be difficult to control the quality on because there are factors beyond your control. For example, I discovered over the years that whenever the flour consistency could radically change from season to season. We didn't use all-purpose flour – we used a very good bread flour that worked great for our dough. But, it's a very good thing there is more than one brand of flour on the market because I had to change brands several times over the years. The brand we were using when the seasons changed became unusable. We didn't discover this until we tried using it! Believe me the first time this happened I thought I was going crazy. But then I went to a food show (that's where tons of vendors and suppliers of food and equipment display their goods) and spoke with a rep from one of the flour companies. He explained this to me and why the flour consistency would change. Oh, here is a cool bonus tip… anytime you go to a food show, try to be there an hour or two before the show wraps up. Many times, these guys and gals DON'T want to take all that stuff back with them, so you can get FREE stuff! I have gotten $30 knives and other cool stuff from vendors doing this, on top of everything else they give away during the show. Don't be afraid to ask – they will just say no if you can't have it.

Speaking of pizza dough, I also discovered that we had to vary the recipe between summer and winter. The water temperature would change. We would have to add more ice during the summer and less during the winter. I also had to discover a better yeast. We used fresh yeast in the beginning because it did a good job raising the dough, but it was inconsistent because it was fresh. Sometimes it would dry out and some batches of yeast activated better than others. I discovered SAF instant yeast. It is a cross between fresh and dried yeast. It worked great, it was consistent, and I was happy to have found it. Consistency and consistent great quality is necessary in any business.

Does all this make sense on the quality aspect? **TIP: Employees must be sold on this.** If you can't sell your employees, you might as well do it all yourself. Or, you will find your business sinking in no time. You really don't want to do it all yourself. As a matter of fact, if you are doing more than a couple hundred dollars a day in sales (as of 2018) you will feel it very quickly. Figure out how to sell those employees. The first thing is that you must set the example in everything you do! Here is a radical example but it absolutely is true. If you want your employees to do a good job cleaning the toilets, then you must do the same.

Service - Customers expect a lot, and deservedly so. They are spending their hard-earned money at your business. They are not buying food. They are buying an experience so remember that when you are dealing with them. Answer the phone as soon as possible when it rings but at least within 3-4 rings at most. When you answer the phone, or you see customers coming in the door acknowledge them. Be happy to see them or hear from them. Smile and be friendly, even on the phone. This shows through. Build rapport with your customers. Get to know them and their families. Their likes and dislikes. Call them by name when you see them.

Show your appreciation for them by being EASY to do business with. Don't keep them waiting for anything. Get their order in as soon as possible. Get their food out as soon as possible without making them feel rushed. When you hand them the check or take their money, ALWAYS thank them and smile. Find ways to make your operation as fast and efficient as possible. Make the customer experience the best it can be. Make EVERYONE happy! Get feedback from EVERY customer. If there is a problem, fix it. Give them a discount. Give them the meal for free. Give them whatever it takes to get them BACK in to see you next time. Employ permanent fixes to issues and bottlenecks. Make sure they don't cause problems in the future. Smooth is the name of the game in servicing customers.

You cannot afford to lose ANY customer. Unless they are impossible to deal with. If that is the case, you may wish to fire them. But do so after much deliberation and ever so gently. Explain that you have done everything possible to make them happy, but you feel that you have failed. Make it about you, not them. Tell them that you cannot see yourself having the capability to serve them in the manner they expect.

Tell them that they may wish to go somewhere else from then on. I probably fired 3 customers in the entire 23 years I had the pizza place. Don't take this advice lightly. You must have PATIENCE for people. Again, you cannot afford to lose customers. If you are not providing excellence to customers, you will lose them. Guaranteed. **TIP: People will buy from you because they ENJOY EVERYTHING about your restaurant.**

Cleanliness: Another success factor in any business but especially in a restaurant is cleanliness. I cannot emphasize enough regarding this point. Employees 'should' be clean-cut and clean. You do not want to offend anyone. They should avoid perfume or cologne. It detracts from the natural smells of your food! If your restrooms aren't clean or are in disrepair, it reflects upon the entire restaurant. It doesn't matter how spic and span the rest of the place is. Restrooms MUST be checked for cleanliness every hour or so when you are busy. Check them as often as possible when you are not busy. Chain restaurants many times have a checklist and times checked for restroom duty. That's a good example and one that you may wish to emulate. Don't make your customers tell you the TP or paper towels or soap is out, or the trash cans are full, either.

You might think the next paragraph is common sense. But go into any mom and pop restaurant and see how many of these issues you can spot. Why are the issues explained here so pervasive? Because complacency strikes. We get so set on seeing things day in and day out.

We never bother to take the 'Martian' viewpoint that a customer has. Familiarity breeds contempt, or in this case, complacency.

With that said, here are just a few of the places to look for cleanliness and other issues that you may not 'see'. But customers will, even subconsciously, and this will devalue their experience in your restaurant.

- Carpeting - stains, tearing, holes. Dirt near the baseboards that the vacuum cleaner missed (and so did the employee!);
- Floors - dirty or stained grout. Areas near the baseboards that have dirt streaks and/or build-up. Dirty, streaked, or build-up on baseboards from the mop;
- Tables - stuck gum under tables. Sticky table surfaces, dirt or build-up on shakers and other containers. Unstable table bases (these are quite annoying!);
- Chairs - dirt or build-up on legs, chair backs and other surfaces. Gum under chairs, tears in the covering, or loose cushions/chair backs. Most chairs are relatively inexpensive - just replace them
- High Chairs and booster chairs - sticky surfaces. Obvious and not so-obvious gunk and dried built-up old food - look at the entire chair

- Booths - tears or holes in the upholstery. Missing stuffing in the upholstery, sticky tables. Gum under the tables, stained upholstery.
- Doors - dirt or build-up at the door bottoms where the mop hits. Build-up on door handles (this happens a lot!)
- Squeaky door hinges and automatic closers. Doors that are difficult or heavy to open or slam shut.

As I said earlier, I bought the business from a family. I celebrated my first day open for business. However, celebration was short. I very quickly realized just what I got myself into. It took me over a year and a half before I made my first real net dollar in the business. That was when I got my food cost under control and started weighing everything instead of just guessing. I lowered prices to more recession-era appropriate pricing. I began advertising on the local radio station that had just changed hands and formats. It went to top 40 pop from country. I advertised for one dollar a spot - 200 spots a month. We also began officially advertising pizza delivery.

We had to work into the pizza delivery. I needed someone to do it but didn't yet have the business to support the service. Given the fact that I worked alone sometimes during the day and the business couldn't afford the extra person yet. We began delivering 5-9 PM when we could afford to hire an extra person. That person doubled as dishwasher/extra prep/delivery driver. I am a big proponent of shoestring financing and if something didn't pay for itself we didn't do it. Pizza delivery, however, soon paid off. We were able to hire the extra person during the day because delivery caught on. People then began calling for delivery during the day.

Several years later, I changed how we hired for delivery. We hired them as subcontractors. They didn't work in the restaurant anymore. They didn't get in the way, which was a problem sometimes. They could do whatever they wanted if it was legal when they weren't delivering. They could even leave and come back. They could hang out, or whatever. They had the understanding that delivery was first come first serve. If they were there when it was ready to take they got to take it. We officially charged a couple of bucks for the delivery. We still had cheap pizza so that worked out great. The driver kept the delivery charge plus their tips. Drivers could make $100 or more over the course of 4 hours less travel expenses, and this was in the 1990's. It worked out for them and it worked out for us because I didn't have to pay more employees. If we had overflow one of the cooks would make the delivery. Or we would call another driver in if it was busy. Plus, we all had a good time, most of the time.

I sold that business in 2005, but not before learning one more big lesson: expansion. In 1990 I was approached by a rep from a shopping center's lessor asking if I wanted to move the pizza business. I was perfectly happy where I was and declined that offer, but the temptation to try a full-service Italian restaurant got to me. Low and behold on Mother's Day 1991 we opened Cannoli's Italian Restaurant. It was a disaster. All of it. But if I had to do it again I would! That's because I learned SO much from the experience that it was still worth it.

We had a decent opening day, but the recession really took its toll on our local economy. Eating out was just not on people's minds. They could not afford it. The pizza business suffered as well, not to mention the fact that a Sizzler opened in July of that year. Talk about Murphy's Law! I closed the doors to the Italian restaurant in October of that year.

One interesting story about the closing - I was very torn about telling the employees. They knew that I was having financial troubles, but closing the doors was another story. I decided to tell them that day. Big mistake - all but one walked out! My last day was spent in absolute misery. Fortunately, I had my awesome wife and the one gal that didn't leave to clean the place up, getting it ready for us to vacate. I did not want to leave it a mess. Besides that, we took some of the equipment with us that I had purchased exclusive of the turn-key lease. We got some nice equipment in the pizza place that I had never had before. Then I fired my manager there for drinking on the job. I also had to let most of the rest of the crew that were doing the same. I went back to managing the place and hired new help. That's never fun but it was necessary. That's called 'cleaning house. '

That year, my first baby boy turned 2 and my newest baby boy had been born the year earlier. I wasn't spending much time at home with the two restaurants, but I had hired a live-in nanny so that helped relieve some of the stress at home. I really missed being at home with my family so when I closed the one place I was very relieved to come home and spend time again. I made up for a lot of that time a couple of years later when I hired a manager at the pizza place and he ran it for me. I got to stay at home for a couple of years and get to be with my kids along with my new baby girl.

LESSONS I LEARNED with my Italian restaurant:
1) Be very aware of the national economy when considering an expansion.
2) Be very aware of the local economy, including new businesses that apply for permits, when considering an expansion.
3) Start small - then get bigger when business can substantially afford it on a long-term basis.
4) Don't hire a known alcoholic to manage your business, no matter how good of a cook he/she is.
5) Don't let the alcoholic manager hire their alcoholic friends to work there. Well this is moot if you observe number 4!
6) I will repeat number 3 - unless you have the numbers to support it, start small. Positivity and reality don't always agree. Add Murphy's Law into the mix and you will have a very hard time of making it work.

Opening a Home-Based Business

A dream that many people have is starting a home-based business. This is a great dream and is worth exploring for many different reasons. It affords many advantages over a brick and mortar business or full-time position. You have to drive to get to those. Increasingly, people work from home these days. Here are the primary advantages to doing that.

1) There is a freedom that a brick and mortar business cannot offer. Excluding meetings and other calendar items, your work schedule can be very flexible. You can easily work early in the morning or late at night. You work whatever schedule works best for you.

2) You don't have to drive very far to get to work. My wife and I tease each other about how far we must drive to get to work. We "drive" from the bedroom across the hallway to the "office".

3) There is a huge potential cost savings. You don't have to pay rent, extra utilities, or employees in the beginning. The latter is true if you have all the skills you need to run the business.

4) A home-based business can be started for very little money. The time you put into it is flexible. Therefore, can be you can work on it off-hours from your full-time job or other endeavor.

5) You can eat at home. You will understand the cost savings from this if you currently work outside the home and don't bring your lunch.

However, a home-based business also has its drawbacks. These include the following.

1) Unless you do otherwise, you never get away from 'work.' Because you are at home and that is where you also work, getting away from work can be a challenge. I recommend that you set up a separate area to work in. Only perform work in that area. The rest of your living area should be used for personal space only. If you do not observe this suggestion, you may find yourself working a lot more than you want. Over time you will feel burned-out. You will find yourself needing a break, possibly at a very bad time.

2) There are more distractions. People that you live with and the distractions they create can easily take you away from your work. These could be accidental or on purpose. But either way they will take you away from work. Again, a separate work area with a closed door will help prevent these distractions from interfering with your work. I have a barky mini-poodle. I always have to keep my office door closed so he does not distract me when I work!

3) It is more work and more expensive to market and advertise a home-based business than a brick and mortar shop. Here are two reasons. First, you might wish to keep your home address private. So in the case of your home-based business you will not be able to advertise your address. You still can, however, register your business on Google Maps using the Google Business page. If you deliver products or services to your customers, you can change to that setting when you set your business up on that page. Be aware though that at this time (as of 2018) Google doesn't really make your business 'seen' outside your immediate local area, no matter what you actually 'say' your service area is. Secondly, there is no signage. An exception is if you are doing business in a home that is also zoned as light commercial. Therefore, all advertising and marketing will need to be done on the Internet and other places outside the home. Look for my online podcast The Travelling Guerrilla Marketer for great low-cost marketing ideas (coming potentially in January 2019)!

4) A potential additional drawback is that you are always around the other people living in your home. This could put a strain on those relationships. Try to make time for yourself to be alone when you need it. Take that time away from work and everyone else. This will help clear your head and give you time to refresh yourself. It was also give the other people a break.

Making the decision to start a home-based business requires a well-thought out strategy. It requires good planning. It also requires the foresight to avoid common problems that can develop with home-based businesses. I am a huge proponent of them. But before you make the commitment, be sure you mitigate all issues before they occur. Consider what could go wrong so you can avoid problems before they occur.

Buying into a Franchise

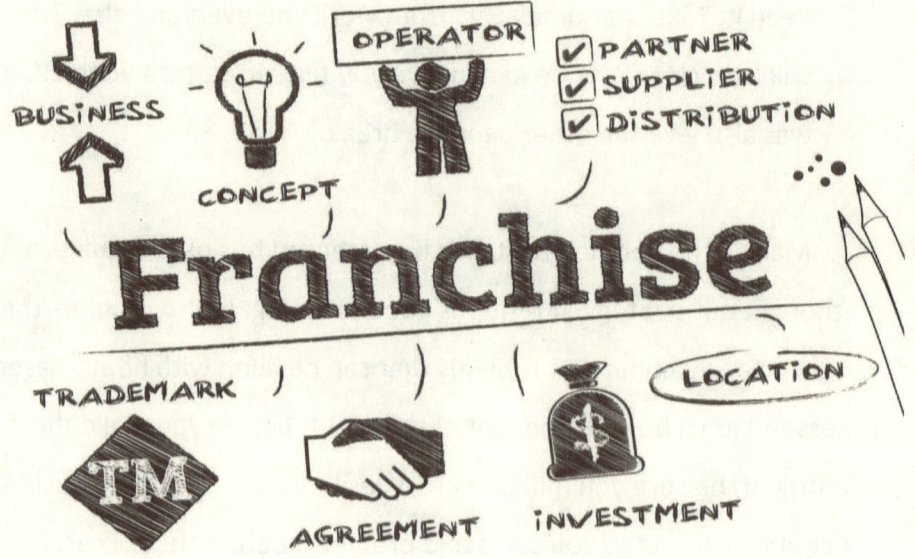

One very popular method for starting a business is by buying into a franchise. Franchises are companies that sell the rights to owning a location or a brick and mortar store based on an already established formula. If you follow their formula in the right location with the right local market you should become successful in the business. Some of the most popular franchises are in the hamburger industry. Think of a national hamburger chain and you will know what I mean.

However, there are franchises available in nearly every industry. It is just a matter of finding one. There is a franchise website link in the resource guide at the back of this book. You will find companies listed by name. In many cases their brochure is listed along with the minimum investment required to buy into the franchise. This minimum amount may or may not include the actual amount to lease a building if it is brick and mortar. Be sure to research each opportunity thoroughly.

Advantages of franchises include buying into an already well-known brand. They usually have lots of company resources behind them. Many times, a brand franchise will put tons of money into marketing in the national markets. This serves to strengthen the brand and benefit the company owned stores as well as the franchise owned stores. Other advantages include consistent products to sell and formulas to follow. They are usually 'stupid-proof' in which anyone can follow. I am not trying to insult anyone. That is a general term that is given to a process or procedure that is specifically spelled out and extremely simple to follow.

Other advantages include having exclusive training opportunities. It also includes the full knowledge and support of the company. The hamburger franchises I spoke of earlier have famous hamburger universities. This is where franchise owners and managers can be sent to train on the company's history, culture, brand, products, and procedures. When you graduate you will know everything you need to know to run your franchise business. Well, at least that is the hope.

Disadvantages to franchised business include the expense of getting started. This is huge in many cases. Another disadvantage is the fact that the company may require you to have access to additional funds in case you need it. The cost of running a franchise can also be very high. Some franchises take upwards of 10 percent and more for their 'rent and royalties' right off the top. Too bad if you can't afford it that month. Their share comes right off the top.

When the company changes its products or services, you must change them as well. If you have a local bestselling product but the company no longer supports it, you are out of luck. Another disadvantage is that in many cases, you must use approved sources for products. If the product isn't approved and the franchisor discovers it, you could be in trouble. The reason is because the company is protecting its brand. They do not want all the franchisees to be selling their own products with varying degrees of quality.

The same goes for advertising. You may be required to pay a certain percentage of your sales to an advertising fund. That fund is pooled together with other franchise stores to advertise in your local market. There may also be other restrictions on when and where you may advertise the brand. This will all be included in your franchise agreement but be sure to ask about these things ahead of time so there are no surprises.

To keep the stores in line with the company's standards, you will typically be assigned a district manager (DM). The DM will visit your store on a regular basis. If you are following the rules you should have no problems. But if you don't follow the rules and the DM discovers issues, you will be subject to some sort of discipline. In worst case scenarios, you could lose your franchise. Be sure to read all contracts with your lawyer prior to signing so you know exactly what you are getting into.

Lastly, just because you bought into a franchise, there is NO guarantee it will succeed. Granted the failure rate is usually MUCH lower for a franchise than an independent. But still you have to invest all that money, especially in a new operation which is unproven in your market. Then it could fail, and you are out all that money. I am not trying to scare you. I simply am pointing out factual information. Again, however, your franchise will (should) do everything it can to mitigate this possibility. They should perform complete market research in your local area to help verify it can support your new store before signing contracts.

Once you find a franchise that you would consider owning, do your research. Contact the company. Learn everything you can about them. Contact other franchisees and get their experiences with the company. How are they being treated? Are they receiving the support they need? Are their company contacts truly helpful or just going through the motions without being helpful? Take tours of stores and see if you really, **REALLY** like them or if you might want to find something else.

Even though this is a franchise, you will want to be sure to follow all the beginning chapters in this book. They will help you verify you are covering your buns regarding the legal aspects. Additionally, you'll make sure that you are doing everything you can to mitigate any problems. Of course, one VERY important question to ask is this. Can you see yourself doing this in 3-5 years, knowing the type of hours and commitment this is going to take? If you answer no, you need to move on!

Long story short - if you want to buy into a franchise, you need lots of money (usually). You MUST do your due diligence to protect yourself, your family, and your future.

Buying Into an MLM

First off, some people think that all MLM businesses (Multi-Level Marketing) are pyramid schemes. I can tell you that MLMs are not pyramid schemes. Allow me to explain. US law has a very specific definition of an illegal pyramid scheme. Pyramid schemes focus strictly on the money aspect of the 'business'. They do not have much of a product to promote, if any at all. Many of them go like this (this is not real, it is just an example). You are sold on the idea of giving $15 to someone. This in turn gives you the opportunity to get $15 from 7 other people - $10 to you and $5 to the person above you that signed you up. When you sign up 7 people, you get $70 and the guy above you gets $35. You in turn get $35 from each of your 7 people that you signed up (if they all sign up 7 individuals). This gives you a total of $315 for your $15 'investment.' The problem is that at some point in time, there will be no more people. The people at the bottom that gave the money will be stuck with no income. Therefore, the people at the bottom lose with no hope of recovering their money. Therefore, it is illegal.

MLM's on the other hand are product or service focused. That is their primary business. Selling the business concept to others, although very important, usually does not occur until after the person being sold to becomes a customer of the business. MLM's occur in all different flavors. There are cleaning based MLM's such as Amway, Melaleuca, and Shakely. There are greeting cards with Send Out Cards. There are legal services with LegalShield (which also provides Identity Theft protection products). Additionally, there are makeup and body care product MLMs such as Mary Kay. There are kitchen products MLMs such as Pampered Chef, and the list goes on and on. Do a Google search for MLM and you will see tons of them.

MLM businesses deserve a special treatment here because there are so many of them. They all promise that you can make lots of money, some with very little work. Many of them sound very, very appealing. Oh, and one more thing - most of them are VERY inexpensive to get started in. This is especially compared to the cost of buying into a well-known franchise. That is their allure and you must be careful about it. Not because they are bad, but because you may end up seeing them as candy. You could end up getting into several them just because they are inexpensive. But that isn't fair to you or to them.

Here is something about MLM's that you should understand. They are a business opportunity just like any other business. You get out of it what you put into it, and that is if you are smart about it. Just as in any business, you can spin your wheels on tasks that don't get you anywhere, and you end up with very little in return. If you are considering investing into an MLM, learn as much as you can about the company and its products and/or services. You are investing into a business. The business can be enormously successful or one that can fail, just like any other business. You should also determine whether a good market still exists in your local area for the MLM you are considering. Most MLM's still have not reached overall saturation. That's where there isn't enough of a market left to make it worthwhile trying to sell that product or service. However, it is still possible to have reached the local market saturation point.

Your upline are the people above you in the organization. The people that would be below you are called your downline. Ask your upline what their thoughts are regarding your local area and whether they think the market is oversaturated. Of course, they ARE invested in the company but ask them for their honest and unbiased opinion. Ask them why they feel that way regarding the possibilities for sales in your local area. Here are 3 very basic considerations to ponder that you need honest answers to when looking at investing into an MLM.

1) You need to find a debt free company with the right vision
2) You should be looking for an easy, "done for you" model where you put your upline to work for you so you can earn while you learn.
3) Lastly, you need a real compensation plan that pays you for all your work... Ongoing commissions are best, even if they start out a little smaller. Also consider how the downline residuals work. Find out how deep you can go in your downline before residuals phase out. Downline compensation plans can be very complicated. Ask your

upline to explain it clearly. Verify that you fully understand it. Ask questions until you're satisfied.

The main point here is that you are making a serious investment. **TIP:** Don't let the fact that it doesn't cost much to get into deter you from putting your best foot forward. Make your best effort every day to work hard. See and talk to as many people as possible to see if they need what you have to offer. Also, there is a right way to sell MLMs and lots of very wrong ways. Remember that your friends and relatives might buy into it just because they want to help you, but that is not your primary market. Many MLMs will try and get you to pester your friends and relatives but they will resent you for it. Find real people that you don't know and help them with their needs. There are lots of ways to do it.

There are some great books that you can read on how to operate an MLM. Research on Amazon and see what you can find on the topic. Lastly, use your support system. Your upline people should be right there with you and be able to answer any questions that you have or get you the answers if they don't have them. Use the MLM's website and learn and discover everything they have for you!

What Do Your Customers See?

1) What DO your current, potential, and new customers/clients/patients see?
2) What logo are you using?
3) Do you have a logo?
4) Do you have a slogan?
5) What is it and does it make sense to a 'Martian?'
6) Where are you advertising?
7) Does the name of your business correlate with what you do, and do people understand it immediately?
8) Are you advertising in the sleaze ball magazine or the uptown one, if any?
9) What image do you portray when you go out in public among potential or current customers? They are all looking at you (sort of).
10) What is your personal online reputation?
11) Have you been in legal trouble?
12) Do you volunteer for Little League or soccer or in the soup kitchens to help people? (I volunteer with our local soccer association and coach and/or referee nearly every year)
13) Are you a prominent figure in your community?
14) What do people find when they do a search for your name in your town or city?
15) Does your business have a website?

16) What is your business's online reputation?

17) Have you taken steps to make it better?

18) Compared to your competitors, does it need to be?

I was told once when I first got into business that people will come around and ask for donations for things such as sports team sponsorships, etc. I was told that I should give to EVERY one of them as I can. I did that over the years and it helps make YOU look good!

19) Does your business have a Google Business page?

20) Is your business listed on hundreds of business directories?

People need to find your business when searching for that type of business in your area if it's a local business.

21) Do you have social media listings for your business?

22) Do you have pictures and videos of you and your employees to put online?

23) Do you have pictures of your products and/or services to put online?

24) Have you researched SEO for your website, so people find you more easily in the search engines?

1) When your customers drive up or walk to your store, what do they see?

2) Do they see a bunch of litter all over the place or do they see a well-kempt parking area, walkways, and landscaping?

3) What does the area smell like? Is it a turn-off or a turn-on, or neither?

4) What do your windows look like? Are they dirty with fingerprints and who knows what or are they clean and shiny?
5) What does the paint look like on the building? Is it old and chipped and stained and faded or is it freshly painted?
6) What does your front door look like? Is it filthy or clean? What about the door handle and other hardware - is it filthy or clean?
7) What does the threshold look like? Is it a hundred years old and broken down or is it in good repair?
8) After the customer opens the door, what do they see?
9) What do they smell?
10) Is it too hot or too cold inside?
11) Are they greeted with a friendly voice or do they feel ignored or even worse, unwelcomed?
12) How quickly do they get service, if appropriate for your business?
13) Do they need help finding something or are they just browsing?
14) Are there signs for what products are in which aisle, or do you make your customers search every aisle for what they are looking for?
15) Are prices openly displayed and easy to find for every product?
16) Can customers see, feel, smell, hear, and/or taste samples of your products if appropriate?

17) Can they experience samples of the products and if so, is there an easily visible sign explaining that and how to do it?
18) Are shopping carts or baskets available if appropriate and are they easily found?
19) Are children welcome or are there childcare services available?
20) Do you have an easy to find and easy to read sign describing that option?
21) Are pets welcome and which kinds? Is there an easy to find and easy to read sign to that effect?
22) Is someone available to assist with customer questions?
23) Does the customer have to look for 10 minutes to find someone when they have a question?
24) Does the customer know your name and better yet, do you know theirs?
25) Do customers feel like they are cared about and that you intuitively know if they need something, maybe even just a glass of water?
26) Does the customer get thanked for coming in to browse, even if they walk out empty-handed, or do they get ignored?
27) If they have a screaming child with them, do you have something to appease them that would be approved by parents?
28) Are checkouts easily visible or does the customer have to hunt for them?

29) Is your list of products and services or your menu easy to read for older folks or do they need their pair of 3X reading glasses to read the headlines?
30) Is the ordering process easy or do customers need to jump through hoops to place an order?
31) Is the checkout process easy and well laid-out or is it difficult to navigate?
32) Do the customers feel valued at the end of the transaction?
33) Is there a buyer's remorse that can set in or do you take steps to mitigate that by sending them a thank you email asking if they have any questions or need any further help, or know they can call and get after-the-sale questions answered quickly and with friendly staff?
34) Are the customers/clients/patients going to rate you 5 stars on Google or Yelp, or not quite?
35) What could you do differently that could bump it up to 5 stars? Be honest with yourself!
36) Do the customers know they can rate you online and that it would help your business if they did?
37) Do you ask customers how their experience was with you and if there is any reason they wouldn't rate you 5 stars on Google?
38) If they loved you, do you ask them to do that?
39) And if they didn't love you, do you offer to discover why and fix the issues immediately?

What do your customers/clients/patients see/hear/smell/feel/taste AND...
Will they want to do business with you again?

According to the Harvard Business Review, it costs between 5 and 25 times as much to gain a new customer versus keeping an existing one. Which would YOU rather do?

Brick and Mortar: Finding the Space

HOME BASED BUSINESSES - YOU CAN MOSTLY IGNORE THIS SECTION :)

If you are going to open a brick and mortar business, you still have a lot of work to do. This work needs to be done after you have:

- ✓ decided what to sell,
- ✓ confirmed you have a local market that will purchase your products and/or services,
- ✓ determined whether you need employees and how many and what their job descriptions will be,
- ✓ looked into your local laws to see what licenses and permits you need,
- ✓ figured out a budget,
- ✓ come up with a business plan,
- ✓ obtained financing,
- ✓ and the myriads of other tasks that you need to do.

WHY did you get into this anyway? FOR THE REWARDS!! :) Now the real fun begins though - you need a place! Home-based businesses of course don't need this, but YOU do!

First, go and talk to a commercial real-estate guy or gal. They can give you the skinny on what's available space-wise given your space requirements. You did take that into account in your business plan, right? They can help work within your budget along with your preferred location in town. Remember these are the 3 biggest contributors to success in a brick and mortar business: location, location, location. Is it worth paying more for a better location? That could depend on your type of business and local competition more than anything. One thing that you can do is research what businesses have come (and maybe gone) in the last 5-10 years in your business niche. See where they were and whether they were successful.

With all the information you now have, your real estate agent can take you around and show you some spaces that might fit your requirements. Here is something else to consider - the available utilities. You must investigate what utilities are available in the spaces you are looking at, and what companies provide them. If you do not do this, you may be in for a very big surprise when you attempt to move into your space. A surprise would not be good.

After you find a space that you like and that will work for you and verified that the utilities service that area and they will all work for your needs, you will negotiate the lease with your prospective landlord. Their representative(s) will probably want to meet with you, so they can determine if you are a good fit. You are also running the same test on them. If you don't feel good about the relationship, you will need to decide. Either accept that it won't be great or move on to greener pastures. Either way, after you meet with the rep and they 'accept' you, you will be presented with a lease. You will want to read that lease cover to cover. Don't worry - the lease will be very one-sided. Trust me I have been there.

Go through the lease with a fine-tooth comb. I strongly recommend hiring a lawyer to help you understand the verbiage. The lawyer will point out clauses that could cause you problems down the road. Decide what things will be deal-breakers and what things you want to change because they will make life easier. This is a negotiation process. You can negotiate until you sign. After that, there is no more negotiation. Everything that is in the lease will be legally enforceable unless a judge or court deems it is not. But you really don't want it to come down to that. Pick out EVERYTHING that you don't like and ask for changes. Just remember - some things will be deal-breakers, some things are just wish-list items. If the landlord says your requested change is a deal-breaker, then you will need to reconsider or give something in return.

In the meantime, while the lease negotiations are underway, get some firm plans together for any remodeling you want or need to do. Don't spend a bunch of money at this point on plans. But you do want to get them in your head and a rough sketch on paper. Contact some contractors and see when they would be available to put together a quote for you. Ask for a rough estimate if possible. Flooring is a big one. If you don't like what is in the space you will need to re-floor the parts of the space you don't like. Look at the existing electrical connections and plumbing. Will that work for you or does it need to change? Are the current rooms going to work or do you need walls put up? Are there any existing code violations? You will wish to speak with your local building inspector about that. Anytime you sign a lease, you are subject to any current laws. The space will no longer be grandfathered. The ADA laws were huge. Any existing business generally didn't have to employ the changes for some time, but new businesses need to comply immediately.

Get a budget put together for the remodeling. Include any new equipment you will need to purchase, hiring and paying employees from the day you sign the lease until you open the store, deposits on utilities, etc. Then take that figure and add 25% minimum to it because everything costs more than you think it will. Unexpected developments can crop up as well. When I moved my business across the street, I ended up spending about $25K more on the remodeling and parking lot renovation than I estimated because things came up that I hadn't planned on. For example, the city required enough rain drainage that we didn't flood out the rear neighbor's lot. That had happened lots of times in the past. I needed a special area built to hold a certain amount of rainwater according to the city code.

Here are some things to request in negotiating your lease. You may not get them, but you can ask:

1) Ask to pay less rent. Depending on how long the landlord has waited for a tenant to fill the space, you may have some leverage on this, especially if the ask rate is higher than the going rate for the area or the area is depressed or has a high vacancy rate. You may have to sign a longer lease to get a lower upfront rate. But hold out as long as possible on this.
2) Ask for the first 3-6 months at half-rent. This is great for a start-up and could be acceptable for a long-term lease (5-10 years).
3) If the first two requests don't work and you think you need it, ask for a lower rent for the first 6 months and tack the unpaid rent on to the last year of the lease, interest free.
4) Ask for a free month so you can get your remodeling completed without having to pay rent.
5) Ask for rent discounts in exchange for permanent improvements to the space.
6) Most rent increases are tied to the national CPI Index. You probably can't change that but verify and fully understand how the costs are calculated. My first landlord didn't increase the rent for 10 years, but then it went up 20 percent.
7) Verify the HVAC and other non-business specific appliance (water heater for example) repairs are covered by the landlord. If not ask for them. They should not be your responsibility.
8) Glass is almost always a tenant responsibility. I have not seen lease terms otherwise so expect that. Same with plumbing.

9) Late charge clauses can be changed in your favor - you can make this a deal-breaker if they don't budge.
10) Make sure you fully understand how to get the money to the landlord every month and what will happen if the rent is late. I had a landlord that lived across the country and I had to MAIL the check every month. I had to plan so it was received by the first of each month. Yes that was fun.
11) If you can afford it, get a lawyer with lease experience involved. You <u>can</u> negotiate the lease yourself but there is a lot of legalize in most of them, so I do not recommend doing it yourself. You could end up in a very deep rabbit hole if you are not careful. At least ask one or more lease knowledgeable friends or relatives to look at it with you.
12) ANY changes in the lease MUST have signatures from you and the landlord's representative. If the changes are not in the lease and they are not signed, they are not valid. Gentlemen's handshakes don't hold water for lease agreements. Get them in writing.
13) Even if you are a corporation, the landlord will still insist on a personal guarantee. That is a good thing for you, not a bad one. Here is why and this is the last thing I will say about leases. If the worst-case scenario comes someday and you are behind by months in the rent because you cannot afford to pay it and you don't know what else to do, a bankruptcy will get you out of the lease. I don't recommend that you do this unless you have no other choice and you need out - badly.

Let's say that you successfully negotiated your lease, you gave some money, all parties signed, and you are ready to go.

Opening Your Brick and Mortar Store

You have your space! Now you can get to the real work that it will take to open your brick and mortar business. You hopefully have drawn up plans for the remodeling and contacted contractors for quotes by now. Follow up on these and begin and complete the work as soon as possible. You are burning valuable time and time is of the essence after you get the keys.

In remodeling the interior, you will generally start high and work down. Like the ceilings for example - get them done first if they need it. Then the walls, then paint, then do the flooring, then any equipment. If you are renovating walls and ceilings, plan on the electrical requirements (including low voltage cables if needed, like ethernet and coax). You don't want to put up sheetrock and then have to retrofit because you didn't plan properly. That isn't fun at all. Also hit your local authorities up and be ready to register your business. You did get a federal employer ID if you are going to have employees, right? Did you also get with your state and local authorities to determine what else you will need? If you are going to sell alcohol or tobacco or firearms you need to get with those authorities as well. Restaurateurs will need to consult with their local health department for policies, procedures, and permits.

Always do the following as you are moving into your space, listed here in no particular order:

1) Get the utilities you need to start remodeling with in your business entity's name immediately and pay the deposits.
2) Put a fresh coat of paint in and on the place after all other remodeling is done but before the flooring, if you are replacing the flooring. Otherwise just paint when you are ready.
3) Pay special attention to the restrooms. If they need new fixtures, put them in. If they are gross, clean them up. Restroom conditions degrade over time. You need to start your business with them in the best shape possible.
4) Put a Coming Soon sign in the window. People are curious and want to know what's coming. This helps to build some momentum for your opening.
5) Discover the local code for signage and order a sign through a reputable company. If you are in a shopping center you will need to get a sign within their specifications. When I opened my Italian restaurant, I needed a sign where each letter was individually lit. That was a VERY expensive sign!
6) Get ALL necessary permits and licenses.
7) Verify any remaining utilities will be on and ready within a week before you open. When I moved my pizza place across the street, I spoke to the phone company 6 months before I moved and requested 4 lines. They assured me that could be done. When it came time within a month before the move, I called them again. They told me I could only have ONE line because all the other

ones were taken on that side of the street.. I was quite unhappy and explained that I needed two phone lines minimum and they had better find a way to get the other line. They did, eventually but before I moved, so I had two lines for me when we moved. Then they came up with the other two within a month after we moved. Lesson here is always follow up and know who you are talking to. A local contact from the utility companies is always the best way to go if you have that option.

8) Plan to have everything else come together within a week before you open. All systems, policies, and procedures in place and tested as best as possible. Employees hired and trained best as possible, walkthroughs completed. Employee handbooks must be completed, and agreements signed. All equipment installed and working, inventory ordered, delivered, and checked in. All customer information designed and printed, POS systems, computers, networks, and Internet up, running, and tested. Website ready for operation, email addresses as needed are in place. Fire extinguishers in place. Septic tank pumped as needed, grease trap pumped as needed. Alarm system in place (as needed) and tested, procedures are fully understood. All local authorities informed, and inspections performed as needed and passed.

The best laid plans of mice and men: everything was ready to go for our restaurant move and reopen date in September 1999. I planned on closing for two days to move all equipment and remaining inventory, get the POS system up and running, and run a test on all the systems. We got everything moved and in place and all equipment was tested and working as it should.

The day we were going to open comes around and the health inspector arrives at 8:00 AM. Checks the hot water in the main kitchen sink. Nope - no hot water. Maybe it just needs to run a moment…… Nope - still no hot water. The dang water heater broke - on the day we were going to open!! Needless to say, I had to make an emergency call at 8:30 AM to my plumber to get it fixed, He arrived at 9:15, fixed the Murphy's law water heater, and the health inspector came back at 10:30. He gave us the clean bill of health and we opened ON TIME at 11:00 AM :) True story.

You Opened Your Business!! Now What?

You want to have a GRAND OPENING!! WOOHOO!!! YOU want to celebrate! WAIT!!! Not so fast :) You have a few things to do first....

Verify that everything is running smoothly. All your equipment must be working properly and can handle 100% capacity. This includes computers and all installed machinery. Same thing with your employees. Is your business like most businesses? Employees will take about 3 weeks to work into a general position. This could be even longer for more specialized or open positions where there are a lot of gray areas that employees need to make their own decisions on.

In restaurants for example, hiring 2-3 employees for every one job required is a good idea for two reasons. First - you will lose employees, sometimes quickly, through shrinkage or if they just don't get it or something else happens. The numbers will dwindle down over the course of a month or two from the opening. Secondly, most everyone will probably be new to the positions and as they get used to the menu and the operation and procedures, things will be inefficient. However, over time the efficiency will increase so the natural decrease in employee numbers will begin to even out with the increases in productivity. That doesn't mean not to hire replacements if you feel they are needed. This was just an explanation of how it will probably work for you.

Lastly verify all processes and procedures that they are as you want them to be. Look at everything that I mentioned over the course of this book including your accounting practices. It all must jive together and work properly. Now is the time to do this. Don't do it after you are so busy you can't see through the forest.

You want to make EVERY customer's experience with your business the absolute best it can be. When a business first opens, everyone is usually new to everything, which causes bottlenecks and time delays in service. You must plan for this and do your best to mitigate any issues that could crop up. See the next chapter on following up with your customers/clients/patients.

The Most Important Piece of Customer Service

In three words: Appreciation. Follow Up. You can do everything right - do what it takes to bring the customer/client/patient into your business, take wonderful care of them, make them feel important when they are there. But if when they (or you) leave they feel like they have been left out in the cold, they may not come back. ALWAYS thank the customer for doing business with you.

In my pizza restaurant, when we saw a customer leave, we thanked them again for doing business with us. I can't tell you how many restaurants, especially chain restaurants, where the customer is not thanked as they are leaving. In other words, they are essentially ignored. This is not good customer service. This is horrible customer service. Although many people may not notice it consciously, you can bet that the difference of the two experiences will be felt at some point, if it wasn't already.

I always thank my customers for everything - for calling, for paying me, for allowing me to help them, for everything they do for us. We get thanked as well! But the point is - make your customers/clients/patients feel appreciated and important to you.

The next thing to do is follow up with them. Tomorrow, next week, next month, three months - those are all good times. Do all of them. Use a program online that follows up with them and verifies that everything is okay, and they do not have any questions or additional needs. In my computer business when it was slow I would go into my business customer's offices and just say Hi and see how things were going. I didn't expect anything - I just wanted to check on them. But many times, it would turn into extra work for me, right then and there. I never asked if they needed anything - I did ask if everything was okay. Do you see the difference in the phrasing of the question? I was not there to solicit, and I didn't want to make a pest out of myself. But it really was a solicitation call :)

If you do use an automation software to follow up with customers/clients/patients you can add valuable tips into your emails, so they are read. The extra goodwill the tips provide makes your people love you even more. Goodwill is awesome - they remember you and the next time they need your service or product you can bet that you will most likely get the call.

If you discover an issue in the follow-ups you must address it quickly. Like immediately - reply to that email or better yet, make the personal call and get the information you need to fix the problem. If you hadn't had sent that follow-up, do you imagine your person would have called you or emailed you on their own? Maybe, maybe not. But those follow-ups elicit that response, and that's what you want! So make sure you do this and do not put it off or forget about it - yes it may elicit a negative response, but who is better to get it, Google or you?

Owner Burnout

We business owners work a lot of hours, especially in the beginning. At first, we are so happy to have our own business, a new business, and we take special care of our new "child." We are there all the time. We oversee everything. We might micromanage everything too. By the way, micromanaging is not something you want to hang onto. Your employees will hate you for it. So be sure to get out of their hair as soon as possible. As soon as you can trust they will do the job correctly and take great care of your customers/clients/patients.

You must take care of yourself. You will work long hours. Take breaks when you can. No, it's not easy to even make time for a break but you must do it. Drink plenty of water. Eat regularly and healthy. Stay away from anything negative in your life. Stay away from alcohol, drugs, gambling, nicotine, negative people. You have enough trouble in your life running your business. All this, without being addicted to behaviors or harmful substances. You need to work your business straight as an arrow. Get a great support team. Take a regular vacation. I used to ask myself if vacations are worth it. In my twenties I didn't think so. I discovered I was wrong. They are super important to take. Take them when you can! They refresh your attitude and super-charge your mind. When you come back chances are you will be revved up and ready to take on the world again.

We start or buy into our business and time goes on. We put in 50, 60, and 80 or more hours per week. We do our best to make our business successful. It takes a toll. We get worn out physically and mentally. We can also get worn out emotionally. We start getting up later in the morning, getting to the office later and wanting to come home earlier. Our patience with people begins getting cut short. We do not feel as enthusiastic about things as we used to. We may be prone to angry outbursts without warning.

This is a sign of burnout. This is not good for you. Your attitude affects everyone around you. It affects your family, your staff, your managers, and most importantly your customers. You need a break. You need it now. You say you can't take a break. Well then you have three choices -

1) Take the break now regardless so you can regain your enthusiasm and come back refreshed and ready to tackle the business problems.

2) Put the break off for a bit but look forward to it and know that you will feel better when you come back. This could put off the burnout for a time, but you WILL need to take that break.

3) Make everyone angry with you and take the possibility that your business will suffer.

It is really your choice - you are the one in charge.

How long of a break should you take? As long as it takes. If you haven't had a true day off in months, one day may do it. Just get away from it - spend time alone and go fishing. Spend it with the wife, the family, friends, go camping. Do whatever you want that's legal for one full day and don't worry about the business. It will still be there when you get back.

It may take a week. A week's vacation once a year at minimum is highly recommended. But it may not be practical. I tend to take the week off between Christmas and New Year's Day plus I will take 10-20 days off every other year. However, I can't say that I don't work during those times because there are always things to do and I tend to be a workaholic. That's me.

Here is the important thing, though - you must learn how to recognize the symptoms, both in you and in your employees. If you are feeling impatient and angry a lot, it could be because of burnout. Take the steps to fix it as soon as possible because not doing so could be detrimental to your business. You MUST find a way to get re-invigorated and EXCITED about your business again (and stay that way)! It is your IMPERATIVE 😊

Billing and Getting Paid

When you are in business for yourself, you oversee everything. One of the most important aspects of this 'everything' concept is that you must make sure you get paid in a timely fashion from your customers/patients/clients. Afterall, money DOES make the world go around, you have your own bills to pay, and besides, that IS why you are in business, right? Great! Now that you have remembered that, let's discuss exactly HOW you get paid for your products and services!

In a typical products business, most everything, if not EVERYTHING you sell should be paid for when the customer receives their product, if not before. Here are some examples:

- Retail store – customer goes into the store, selects their products, proceeds to the checkout and pays for their goods.
- B to C (Business to Consumer) online products store – customer goes online, browses for their products, moves the ones they want into the 'cart' and proceeds to checkout. They pay for their order with a card or other electronic means, and the products get shipped.
- B to C Online services – customer goes online, selects the service(s) they want, moves them to the cart, and orders the services, preferably paying for them prior to or in conjunction with scheduling the service. However, there are lots of cases where this is not practical. Keep reading 😊

Real-world services – this is where the payment process gets a bit murky and sticky. Here is why – it is customary for customers/clients/patients to NOT pay for their services UNTIL the services have been rendered.

- Doctor's/dentist's office or health-care facility – you get seen, and you typically pay (or submit to insurance)
- Beauty salon/barber shop – you get your hair done and then you pay (remember the tip!)
- Accountant's office – you get your bookkeeping or taxes done, and you pay when you receive your reports
- B to C plumber/electrician/other home-service specialist – technician/repairman comes to your home or office, renders their service, and you pay them before they leave, UNLESS other arrangements have been made. NOTE I said UNLESS. That is extremely important.
- B to B (Business to Business) ALL Services – YOU as the service provider must determine the terms for this. Many businesses are not willing to/not used to/cannot for whatever reason pay WHEN the services are rendered. For many types of services, you CAN STILL collect your money WHEN the service is rendered. HOWEVER, you MUST communicate these terms PRIOR to rendering the services. If you do not do this and the business cannot/will not pay when you are done, it is your problem. Seriously – so make sure you ARE communicating your payment terms when setting up your service calls. Some businesses will even pay for service ahead of time, getting a discount for purchasing 'blocks' of time. Consider this route but remember after you have spent the money (if you didn't save it or put it into a special account for that purpose) you still must provide the service.
- B to B advertising services — usually paid monthly after the month the service takes place. However, this can be a problem because paying for advertising is about the last thing a business owner will pay for when things are financially tight. Sounds kind of counter-intuitive but consider what else must get paid. Advertising is far down the priority payment list. Consider different payment terms for new or floundering business. Don't

be afraid to get full monthly payment up front. Will you lose the customer? Maybe – but it really is better than having to keep after them for payment month after month or worse, having to write it off as a loss.

- B to B long term or larger projects such as websites, construction projects, etc: Typical terms include 50% down and 50% upon completion, or a third down, a third halfway through the project, and a third upon completion. Or half down and payments throughout the project term Essentially, YOU set the terms, but make sure they are terms YOU can live with. Don't set terms for your business and then not be able to live with them. For example, if you need to pay an employee half the project amount, make sure you have enough cash flow to get through the project. Accounting for (there's that 'planning' word again) unexpected delays will also be extremely beneficial.
- Recurring billing (service contracts, ongoing services rendered, etc): Use software that sends the invoices for you AND sends automatic reminders to non-payers (see the resources section for a suggestion). This way you will not have to worry about getting the invoices out and you won't feel 'badly' about having to bill people (yes, I do that sometimes too and then I don't get paid, which is bad for ME!).

FINAL WORD: Protect yourself! Do not trust businesses to pay you. I am not saying they won't – just don't believe they will. Believing this will get you to set the best terms for yourself. For example, never present a finished project without getting final payment either prior to or upon presentation, unless you have good reason to believe that you won't get taken for a ride. Be smart about money and getting paid for your valuable products and services. No one else is looking out for YOU but YOU.

Accounting for Your Business

We can get so caught up in the day-to-day operations and running our business. We may forget a very important aspect of the business - accounting for it. This in both in literal and figurative terms. It is something that you need to either do yourself or hire someone to do it for you - once a month. It needs to be done each month for several reasons. First, because you will have reporting that needs to be made and turned into your tax authorities, along with any payments that are due to them for the latest time period. NOT submitting those reports and payments will result in additional penalties and interest being assessed (that you CAN'T get out of). Do yourself a huge favor and don't get behind! Secondly and even more importantly, for your own information. The reports that you get will be invaluable to you in making new decisions regarding what direction the business is headed, and if a change in direction (whether major or minor) is warranted.

How do you account for your business? It starts at the most basic level. Each transaction that your business makes must be recorded. This is whether you purchase a good or service or sell a good or service. Believe me, you want to record these transactions sooner than later. Waiting will cause a train wreck of transactions that need to be recorded all at once. Also, the time that passes makes us forget what they were for and other important information regarding them!

What is the best way to record these transactions? Use computerized software. Use a point of sale system for your customer transactions (AKA POS Systems) and accounting software for your outgoing transactions. Even better, use the same software, or software that interfaces with each other, for BOTH types of transactions. I use online software called Xero for mine. It works great, it is fast, provides great reporting, and has many advantages over its competitors. It also interfaces with many 3rd party apps that provide additional functionality.

Here's a tip regarding point of sale software. Unless your business is a general brick and mortar business, it will probably require a specialized point of sale or other tracking software available from any one of several 3rd party vendors. Be sure to investigate the software company thoroughly before signing on. Know exactly what you are getting into. Most companies sell their software for a very expensive price. Plus, you are required to sign onto their annual agreements. These agreements provide a certain number of hours of support as well as upgrades to the software, generally all-inclusive in the price you pay. Again, be sure you know exactly what you are getting yourself into. Also, determine what accounting software it can interface with, if any. Another piece of online software you could look into for your needs is Zapier. This software doesn't do anything by itself. What it DOES do is help different pieces of software interface with other pieces of software. This gives each software package additional capabilities that it doesn't have by itself.

I strongly recommend that you hire someone to do this for you. Unless you really like doing it or you are a glutton for punishment, hiring someone will be much easier :) A professional will make sure things are done correctly. They are generally liable for any mistakes in reporting, unless you submitted incorrect figures to them. That IS the purpose for the software I suggested, right? A bookkeeper can do your books for you every month. They will submit your reporting to the tax agencies, and even write the checks or submit online payments for you. A tax professional such as a public accountant or a Certified Public Accountant can help you with your taxes every year. They get more training and are generally more knowledgeable about the tax code. In the US, corporate tax filings are due on March 15th and personal tax filings are due on April 15th unless those days fall on a weekend or holiday, in which case the date will generally be extended to the next business day. Payments are due on a schedule that the government determines. Be sure to consult with your tax professional regarding payments or you could become a victim of additional penalties and interest!

Here is another very important secret - you need to know if you are good with money or bad with money. That means - do you spend it as it comes in, no matter how much or how little it is? Or are you more likely to manage it well? I admit it - I am one of those people that is typically NOT good with money. Well I try to be good with it, at least some of the time! If you are more like me in terms of money management, try to let someone else manage your money for you. A trusted advisor is a good person to help with that. Take a salary every week for yourself (with taxes taken out of your paychecks), establish a personal budget, and stick to it. Put some money away for vacation every week. **Keep the business's money and your personal money separate - commingling of funds is a VERY bad thing to do!**

You need to understand there are two resources that we must always juggle, and this concept becomes even more important in business. Can you guess what they are? Time and money. That's it. They are both finite. But unlike time, money can be increased, or decreased. Like time, money needs to be managed effectively so we can make the most out of it. What can you do to manage those two resources more effectively? Time management and money management. Look those terms up on the Internet and discover how you can more effectively manage them.

Here is a little piece of philosophy I came up with in terms of the money and time resources dilemma - - in business you will generally have an excess of one or the other, sometimes neither of both, and rarely an excess of both. However, when you become more successful, **your goal is to have an excess of both**.

Selling Your Business

The day may come when you want to sell your business. Before I go further, here is one thing that I learned - if you try to sell your business when it is distressed (losing money) you will not get much for it. In fact, you will lose more money, IF you can find a buyer for it. It is a really difficult situation to be in, and one that I was in many years ago. I really wanted out of the pizza business - I was losing money and I didn't know how to make money - we were in this recession and it was just awful. I cried many nights at home and I wanted out. One day a guy came in that owned a place in the town not far from us and made me an offer. It was a lowball offer that wouldn't have even paid what I was in debt for. I told him no. I almost felt insulted, but most of all I felt stupid because here he was in a place that he could buy my place and I was in a much worse place. What that did, however, was gave me the resolve to figure out how to make it work. And I did.

With that said, if you can possibly find a way to make your business work, and believe me it could take time, and you really need to honestly know if your product or service is viable and in-demand AND is not in an oversaturated market AND the economy is sustainable, then do your best to do that. Give your customers what they want but be certain you can do it for a price that makes a profit. It is horrible to put all that time and effort into a business that makes no profit. Reinvent the business if you have to but be sure not to alienate your current customer base should you decide to do that. That is, if you have a customer base to speak of.

Selling a business is tough business, and chances are you will not get as much for it as you feel it is worth, especially if your business is in the "not making too much money" category like mine was for many years. In my computer business in 2007, I approached a competitor and 'sold' him my business for $10K including the inventory, blue sky, name, and phone numbers. Why? Because I desperately wanted out and was willing to do anything to get out. I was making a little money, but it would not pay my bills. So, I sold it cheap.

The REAL way you want to sell your business is when it is making a ton of money in a booming economy - then you will probably get at least close to what you want for it and go off and start another business. Just make sure you follow the good common-sense principles that you learned from this book! How old should your business be before you consider selling? The minimum is really about 2-3 years if it is making decent money, but for argument's sake it should be closer to 5+ years. You will have a long-established track record of success at that point and can show the income that proves the worth of the business. Some business owners will start a business and turn it over very quickly, then do the same thing with the next business. I guess you could call them serial entrepreneurs, but not business owners :) If that's your thing, then that's great! But that's not really what this book is about.

How much should you sell it for? That really depends on whether you have machinery, equipment, and other tangibles or if you only have intangible blue sky (the value ascertained from the annual net income). I would strongly recommend setting an appointment with a commercial business broker (or three) to discuss the value of your business, how saleable it is, and what kind of timeframe he/she thinks it would take to sell the business. Verify references and reviews of the broker - you don't want to get involved with anyone shady. Whether you actually list with that broker will be up to you. Their terms ARE negotiable so do negotiate for the best terms - rate, listing time, and whether they have the sole rights to the listing. Just remember that if they have greener pastures elsewhere, your listing will not be given priority.

What about the 'books?" I never kept the '2' sets of books that I heard a lot of businesses do, so I don't have that information available - I always reported my income because this did two things for me - I slept well at night and when it came time to sell I didn't have to worry about cooking up some story about how much I really made versus how much I said I made. Oh yeah and the other benefit is that the other employees saw ME ring up everything which impressed upon them to do the same thing. I have seen restaurant and other business owners put money in the register and not ring it up on the register. I knew what was going on but I never was a party to it and I don't recommend you do it either. When it comes time to sell your business, your 'books' will be your books and you won't have to worry about that, either.

You will have to give some concessions when you sell your business. One of them is a training period. The person purchasing your business may know nothing about it. You will want to give them their best chances of success by providing the best training you can. This generally will last for no longer than a month. Then you can just be available for an occasional question that comes up. Or if a previous customer has a question that the new owner does not know the answer to.

Another concession may be financial terms such as taking payments for a period of time after the closing date. In this case you will need to have a promissory note signed by the buyer for the full amount, and mark it paid or give some piece of paper stating it has been satisfactorily paid. The terms can be level (a fixed amount of money paid every month for a fixed amount of time until fully paid) or a balloon (a fixed amount of money every month for a certain amount of time and then a balloon for the last payment), or a rate based as a percentage of sales for a period of time. The type of note you take will depend on what you want to do, and what the purchaser is willing to pay.

Just remember that everything is negotiable, and you want to make sure that you get what you feel is fair. The other person wants the same thing for them, so remember that too. Get a contract for the sale and get a lawyer. If you use a broker they will supply all that, which is the nice thing about using a broker. If you don't you will be on your own. Either way you will need a lawyer to look over your contract, make sure it is legal, and there are no holes.

Final Words - The Best Advice You May Ever Get

I could have condensed this book into this one chapter, but what fun would that have been? Seriously though, if you don't get anything else out of this book, please at least tear these pages out of the book or copy or print them (you have my permission) and put them in places where you will see them, read them, and remember them. These are turbo-charged information items that will help you get the most out of your business.

1) **Make your business easy to find on the Internet and the real world.** If you don't have a sign or don't promote your business, no one will know about it. YOU have to be the biggest proponent of your business - tell everyone about it. You may not need to sell it by making cold calls (you hope!) - it will probably sell itself to the right people if the product or service is needed, you have established trust, the quality is great, and the price is right. But if the right people don't know about it, then you will not have a business. Obscurity is you and your business's worst enemy.

2) **Make it EASY to do business with you every step of the way!** Look at all of your processes from your advertising and signage to the first contact process through the payment process. Go through them as you the owner, then go through them as a customer. Where are the hang-ups and bottlenecks? What didn't

go as smooth as it could? Whenever you change your processes do exactly as I stated here. I learned in my pizza business that when there were bottlenecks, it generally was a process issue and NOT an employee issue.

3) **Answer your phone, answer your door, answer your emails whenever possible.** Answer promptly and professionally. One of the things that I hear repeatedly in my businesses is that people APPRECIATE my professionalism. I don't freak out over problems – I have a can-do attitude and I am always positive, even under the worst circumstances. Do I get impatient? YES! But I take a breath (I excuse myself to use the restroom if needed) and do my BEST to remember why I am in business - to provide solutions to their problems!

4) **Got a website? Your phone number should be PROMINENTLY displayed on EVERY page**, including in VERY large font at the top of your home page. Your phone number should also be displayed in the 'Description' field of your website so when Google displays your listing, it will show up with the phone number as well. Ask your web designer or call or visit MY business at G6 Web Services at https://g6webservices.com for help on this.

5) **If you have customers or potential customers trying to contact you, let them!** I can't tell you how many people will just go down their list of businesses to call and hang up as soon as they get the voicemail greeting to move on to the guy or gal that WILL answer their phone. I had a call today from a now new customer that told

me I wasn't the first on his list, but I was the first to answer the phone! I know it is not easy to answer the phone every time or by the 2nd or 3rd ring, especially in the service business. But - find a way and do your best to answer every call. Every missed call could also be a missed customer/client/patient.

6) **Keep a close eye on your front-facing employees.** Okay, really keep a close eye on ALL employees but especially your front-facing ones. They will make or break your business in their attitude. I know a CPA that is the nicest guy in the entire world. He hired this woman and positioned her in the office to front-face his clients. She was a great worker and very knowledgeable about accounting, but with her attitude toward people, she really needed to be in the back office. I discussed the matter with him and he said that I wasn't the first to point it out. Therefore, the back office is where she went. Don't ignore these things - remember these people represent your company, your brand. People buy, or not buy, based on feelings. Unfriendly people will leave a very bad feeling. Remember the Golden Rule when doing business.

7) **Spend smart money to make money.** I recently got off the phone with a real-estate agent friend of mine (and he is a client) that tells me he wants to save money on his marketing. He spends $550 a month ($6600 a year) on a marketing platform. He sold $4M (yes that is 4 million) dollars of real estate last year between all of the leads coming from this particular platform. He made

120K on a $6600 marketing investment. He was thinking about dropping them to save money (seriously) - what do you think I told him? I told him not only would he be nuts to drop them, but he needs to be looking at other venues that can give him that kind of return!! (They ARE very rare) However, I did tell him to DUMP any marketing platforms that haven't returned anything for him in the last 6 months. THAT'S where you save the money!!

8) **When starting your business or making changes, ALWAYS budget 20% (or more) more than the figure you arrive at.** Everything always costs more than we think it is going to. When I moved my restaurant, I NEVER thought the money expenditure would be over! It finally was, and I ended up spending about 20% more than I initially had budgeted. Fortunately, business was really good at the time and I was able to make that work.

9) **When business is slow, spend your time personally marketing your business.** If you are like me, you may get depressed when business is slow and get worried about paying the bills. Over the years I have discovered that my psoriasis really acts up when I am worried about money. But trust me - you can spend a lot less energy marketing your business than you spend worrying about it. How? Guerrilla Marketing is where it is at. If you don't know what it is, discover it - it could save your bacon in many ways. Every place that you are NOT when your prospects are looking for your niche is one more customer you WON'T get. Be EVERYWHERE! I am working on a free podcast out called the **Traveling Guerrilla**

Marketer – I hope to have it on the Internet after December 2018 so check it out - you will get TONS of ideas to help you get more business!

10) **When you need additional business, look to your past customers/clients/patients.** Is it slow? Email, call, or visit your previous customers. Ask how everything is going, if they were happy with the service/products they received from you, and if they need anything. It doesn't hurt to ask, and I can guarantee you that if you are taking great care of your customers to begin with, you WILL find that some of them need or desire something from you when you contact them. Better yet, build a continuity program for your customers/clients/patients. Build extra value into a package for a special price that will all but guarantee they will keep coming back, as long as you do your job and keep them happy :)

11) **What's the best way to convert cold hopefuls into raving fans?** FREE SAMPLES!! Not too many companies do this anymore because it can take a lot of resources. But done right you can give a great amount of value for no charge, show your potentials your expertise, and gain new customers quickly. This works especially well for restaurants. If you have a lot of foot traffic, stand outside your door and hand out bite size samples, just like Costco. If you don't have foot traffic, look on the Internet for local businesses and pick a 'winner' - call them up and tell them they get a free lunch worth so many dollars. Send over a menu and let them

choose. Put your best foot forward! Service businesses can do the same thing - when people call you, give them the info they are asking for, for no charge. When they find they can't do the job themselves, you will get the call.

12) **KNOW who your customers are and where to find them.** You could spend a MILLION dollars on all kinds of marketing but if you are trying to sell ice cream to people that hate ice cream (I can't imagine this, can you??!!) you won't sell any dang ice cream!

13) **SUPPLIERS: Play them against each other to get the best deals!** When I was in the pizza business, I would never use just one supplier. This way I could compare prices and get the best deal. Salespeople DO have wiggle room – if that supplier is overpriced compared to another, tell your person – chances are many times they can beat the other guy.

14) **PARTNER WITH OTHER BUSINESSES** – many times you can trade reviews with your business partners and friends – you give them a great review, then they will give you a great review. This works not only on review sites, but on social media like LinkedIn! How else can you partner with other businesses? Consider what businesses you could run cross-promotions with. Hand out each other's cards, give discounts to each other's business for using the other business, etc. All kinds of great things – just reach out and touch someone 😊

15) **Before you do ANY extra marketing for your business, make sure EVERYTHING is RIGHT with your business!** I said this in another

chapter, but I am saying it again because it is SO important. PLEASE PLEASE PLEASE do yourself the favor of keeping up with this concept. Not just today or tomorrow – but always.

16) **Step back and look at the big picture on a regular basis.** Where are you now, where did you come from 6 months ago, 1 year ago, 2 years ago? Are you making progress toward your goals? Do you have your goals clearly laid out and written down? Where do you see yourself in 6 months, a year, 2 years, 5 years, at retirement? The only way to get there is to keep the big picture in mind and work toward it on a regular basis. Sometimes we need patience. Sometimes we need a kick in the butt. But we decide and oversee where we want to go, when we are going to get there, and how we are going to get there.

17) **Take better care of yourself.** (WARNING - DEEP DARK TRUTHS EXPOSED HERE) Want to be in top shape for your business? If you don't get enough sleep, get enough to eat, get enough water to drink, don't have a good homelife, don't get a regular vacation, or abuse or overwork yourself to the point of exhaustion, you will not be in top shape to run your business. If you sit in a chair all day in your business, get up every hour for 5-10 minutes and stretch and walk around. Take a good walk every day. Go to the gym. Eat better - stay away from sugar as much as possible. Take a full day to yourself at least once a month or more often if you can. If you smoke cigarettes, then quit (I quit cold turkey when I was 34). If you are horribly overweight find a way to lose it. I just

lost 50 lbs. last year and feel so much better! If you gamble, find a way to stop (by the way, many small business owners have lost their businesses due to a gambling addiction - don't let it be you). If you do drugs, find a way to stop. Your teenager years are over. If you have a business, it demands you to be 100% responsible to it. I have a great friend that was hooked on meth for many years while he had a business, and he lost it because the drugs took over his life. I don't gamble, and I don't do drugs. *Is taking better care of yourself a difficult thing to do? In some cases, hell yes! Only you can make this decision, though, but believe me when I say this - the ONLY way you can be dedicated to your business in the way that IT needs you is to take care of yourself FIRST.*

18) **Use great time management techniques as discussed in this book.** If you enjoy spinning your wheels everyday speeding around like a Ferrari on a race track but going nowhere regarding your goals, then please do not use time management techniques. However, if that idea does not appeal to you, then do yourself a huge favor - get and use them every day. Set your overall goals, write down a timeframe for them, then determine the tasks to reach them, and write down the tasks everyday so you can reach those goals.

19) **Look at and be aware of global, national, state, and local news at all times as it pertains to the economy or your specific industry.** When we were in the tv repair business, we were told that digital signals were coming, and the FCC was going to re-purpose the old

VHF and UHF bands (which they did). We also saw that LCD and plasma televisions were coming. We looked at how that was going to affect the TV repair business. It wasn't good for us. We knew TV repair days were limited so we took steps to mitigate the effects. We got out of the business while the getting was good!

20) **Lots of salespeople will email, call, or come into your store.** I made mistakes by buying from some of them. Other times I made good decisions by buying from others. Here is a rule to live by – never buy on the same day you meet a new salesperson. Sleep on it. Consider the positives and negatives of the transaction. Explore alternatives by researching on the Internet and/or local phone book. Research the company - look for online ratings and reviews. Most professional salespeople are not local – they are out of town – so ask. You are a local business - try to keep your money local if you can…. After considering your research, make your decision and get back to the salesperson. Yes, some of them will tell you it is today's special (the law of scarcity), but consider this – you didn't even know about the product before they came in, so are you worse off by saying no? And what salesperson in their right mind wouldn't give you the same deal tomorrow? If they don't, it wasn't worth it to begin with.

21) **WARNING: There are LOTS of scams and less than charitable charities that will try their best to get your money** – the Fraternal Order of Police, this charity, that Handicapped organization, etc. If you want to consider donating, research them online and see

what percentage of funds actually GOES to the benefactors of the charity. If it is less than say 60 percent, I would seriously consider not donating. And those Fraternal Orders of Police etc? The majority are not going to benefit your local police or sheriff department! Give only at your own behest, not theirs.

22) **You will get asked to give money by Girl Scouts, Boy Scouts, and any other charity organization.** The piece of advice I got when I first started out was to give something to everyone. This way you don't get people upset with you. I had lots of fun sponsoring a bowling team for $25 a year. They also came in to eat once or twice a month, so it more than paid for itself. Any team, any organization that came in got something from me before they left. Good for them, and good for me.

Great Resources

There are tons of great resources out there, many of them for free or low cost, that will help you own and operate your business. Note that unless specified, I am not an affiliate and do not make a commission if you sign on. Here are just some of them:

1) The United States Small Business Administration (SBA) has tons of free material to help you in your business. Go to their website at https://www.sba.gov/course/ to learn more about business, and to https://www.sba.gov/writing-business-plan to get started writing your business plan.
2) SCORE is an extension of the SBA and its purpose is to further help small business owners succeed. Local chapters exist all over the United States. They will assign you a mentor if you would like one, that specializes in what you want help with. Their website is https://www.score.org/ where additional resources will help you in your quest.
3) https://www.usa.gov/start-business?source=busa is an amazing resource for further US Government information on minority and veteran owned businesses and links to other government resources. It is a great place to start and work in if you are lost in the myriad of information out there.

4) Looking for business form templates? Tons are available for free at this time at http://forms.entrepreneur.com/categories/applications
5) The site https://www.franchiseopportunities.com/ has a searchable list of franchises by industry and you can browse until your heart's content.
6) Inc.com has a great article on how to use this strategy to build your business on the side while working your full-time job https://www.inc.com/jeff-haden/the-side-hustle-how-to-guide-10-rules-for-side-hustle-success.html
7) Crowdfunding has become hugely popular in recent years for doing anything from paying unexpected medical bills to starting a business and funding other projects. Although the ultra-popular Kickstarter cannot be used for business specifically, others can be. Inc online has a blog article with a list of sourcing for you at https://www.inc.com/magazine/201111/comparison-of-crowdfunding-websites.html
8) Xmind Zen: This is downloadable software to help you organize and stay organized. They call it mind-mapping because you can map your thoughts quickly and easily in flow-chart patterns. It is currently free in that you never have to register it. It is available at https://www.xmind.net/zen/#overall
9) Hubspot Free CRM: This free online CRM works great for new companies that need salespeople and need to keep track of their leads. Of course they sell very expensive add-ons and other

software, but for basic, this will work great. It is available at https://www.hubspot.com/products/crm

10) Xero: This online accounting software is available at https://www.xero.com - as of this writing they offer a free trial and a very reasonably priced program that can be upgraded as you grow. The automatic recurring invoice capability along with reminders for non-payers is worth the subscription price by itself!

11) Zapier: An online software package that integrates different software packages together giving them additional capabilities (call Zaps) they didn't have by themselves. Go to https://www.zapier.com for details. As of this writing they provide a free trial.

12) Learn how to speak in public. Overcome your fears. Join Toastmasters - their info is at https://www.toastmasters.org/

13) Need a superb email contact manager and CRM (Customer Relationship Management System)? There are many out there, but one sticks out as the best, by far. Check out Active Campaign's benefits and features at https://g6webservices.com/top-benefits-of-active-campaign/

14) Would you like to learn the real secrets to branding and other aspects of marketing your business? Join the member's area at https://www.g6digitalmarketing.com – then become a Silver Member with the code FREESILVER and you will get my entire course on Branding and other bonus materials for no charge, just for buying this book.

15) Give back to your community and get known for what you do while you are doing that. Join your local Kiwanis, Lions, or Rotary club. Join your local chamber of commerce. Become involved in their activities and help them in any way you can. Joining isn't enough - you must get involved and get known. Find any other way to get involved in your community that you can. Work a soup kitchen or other place where they feed the homeless two hours a week. Coach a youth sport. It will make you feel great and you will be serving your community. *95 percent of people do not volunteer their time for the community they live in – they claim they are too busy with their lives, but it is all a matter of priority. Can you be a helper in your community for just a couple of hours a week?*

Thank you so much for reading this book!!

Would you like more information, more insight??? Call me personally at 800-590-2085 so we can talk! I offer business courses and coaching programs designed to help maximize your business investment, help you run your business more efficiently and effectively, and help you get what you want more out of life!

www.ingramcontent.com/pod-product-compliance
Lightning Source LLC
Chambersburg PA
CBHW030653230426
43665CB00011B/1080